One-Day Macramé

A Beginner's Guide to Quick, Easy & Beautiful
Hand-Knotted Home Décor

one-Day Macramé

Mariela & Carolina Artigues

Creators of Port Macramé Studio

PAGE STREET
PUBLISHING CO.

PAGE STREET
PUBLISHING CO.

First published in 2023 by
Page Street Publishing Co.
27 Congress Street, Suite 1511
Salem, MA 01970
www.pagestreetpublishing.com

Distributed by Macmillan, sales in Canada by The Canadian Manda Group.

27   26   25   24   23   1   2   3   4   5

ISBN-13: 978-1-64567-736-9
ISBN-10: 1-64567-736-2

Library of Congress Control Number: 2022945413

Cover and book design by Rosie Stewart for Page Street Publishing Co.
Photography by Katta Tubio, Marieta Deya, Maru and Caro Artigues

Printed and bound in the United States of America

Page Street Publishing protects our planet by donating to nonprofits like The Trustees, which focuses on local land conservation.

TO THE LOVES OF OUR LIVES, OUR KIDS.
TO OUR SUPPORTIVE AND LOVING MOM AND DAD.

TO YOU, FOR GIVING VALUE TO HANDMADE ART.
AND TO ENTREPRENEURS—GO ON BELIEVING
IN YOU!

contents

Macramé & Us
IT'S ALL ABOUT SIMPLE KNOTTING

Welcome to our world of macramé! Macramé is definitely in vogue again, especially when it comes to home décor. We think this revival came about because so many people all around the world started creating magnificent pieces and generously sharing them on social media, which inspired other makers to give it a try!

What makes macramé so eye-catching and popular is its versatility and that it is an art form that is easy to begin, not only for experienced makers but also for anyone who feels curious about it. That's why our motto is, "It is not about knowing a thousand knots. It is about being creative with some of them!" That is the essence of our work.

As crafty girls and décor lovers, macramé pieces obviously caught our attention and we were immediately immersed in a world that would bring us a lot of satisfaction and personal growth. Like most makers, we are self-taught and figured it out as we went along; we soon found a new passion making decorative pieces for our homes. Macramé reached us in a moment in which we were searching for a new direction in our lives. We were moving abroad, miles away from our

homes and it played a very important role in keeping us optimistic and grateful during the pandemic. The beauty of simplicity guided us to find a style, and we soon realized that we wanted to share our knowledge with a world that was going through such a complicated time.

One-Day Macramé is a quick guide to introduce you to the amazing world of macramé through simple projects using the most basic knots, which will open the door to creativity and unique, hand-knotted pieces.

Each section of this book is carefully crafted to help you feel comfortable while beginning your knotting journey. As a starting point, we suggest that you make one of the projects included in the chapter "A Blank Canvas" (page 41), so you can practice the knots in a small, very simple piece. After that, you will be more than ready to tackle any project from the following chapters.

Practice makes perfect, so we assure you that you will become a skillful maker with this book. Thanks for being here; we hope you enjoy the journey!

BEFORE YOU START
HELPFUL THINGS TO KNOW &
FAQS FOR BEGINNERS

Once your fingers get wrapped up with macramé cords, you will fall head over heels in love with this art! But before you jump in, there are some helpful things we want to share with you to make it a more pleasant path.

From our experience in teaching the art of knotting, most beginners are doubtful about the same things. So, if this is your first encounter with macramé, or if you struggled with it at first and want to give it another chance, you are surely eager and full of energy to start your first project! Our aim in this section is to help you avoid and overcome some of the common issues that tend to arise in the process.

WHAT DO YOU NEED TO START KNOTTING?

Basically, all you need is some cord and a good pair of scissors! This is what makes macramé so spectacular: using simple materials to achieve stunning pieces. Depending on the project, you will also need a few other elements such as a dowel and/or wooden or metallic rings.

Most macramé projects require a large amount of long cords, so we suggest you work with them while they are hanging down. This will not only simplify your work, but it is also more comfortable. We love to use a clothing rack, but don't feel the need to rush out and buy one; this is not necessary to start! You can find a place at home to hang them from—for example, a curtain rod or the back of a chair.

WHICH TYPES OF CORDS/ STRINGS ARE BEST FOR BEGINNERS?

There are different types of cords and materials you can use to knot. For beginners, we suggest 3mm 3-strand twisted cotton cord and 3mm or 5mm single-twist cotton cord. These thicknesses and textures are more versatile and make for easier knotting than thinner or thicker ones. They highlight designs, making them more appealing. And what's more is that they are the most commonly used in the majority of macramé projects.

WHERE IS THE BEST PLACE TO BUY MACRAMÉ CORD AND OTHER SUPPLIES?

Macramé is so in vogue that many artists have also become macramé cord suppliers. Here we will share with you some of those who, apart from being great artists, also sell beautiful and high-quality materials to work with.

CLOVER CREATIONS

UK, international shipping
Clovercreationsuk.com

CREATEAHOLIC

Sweden, international shipping
https://linkpop.com/createaholic

CAREFREE CORDS

USA, shipping USA and Canada
msha.ke/carefreecords/

THE IVY STUDIO

UK, international shipping
Theivystudio.co

JAC HOME HEART

Australia, shipping to Australia, New Zealand and USA
linktr.ee/jachomeheart

THE LARK'S HEAD

USA, international shipping
msha.ke/thelarksheadshop

CREADOODLE

The Netherlands, European shipping
Creadoodle.com

LOTS OF KNOTS

Canada, international shipping
linkpop.com/lotsofknots

MARY MAKER STUDIO

Australia, international shipping
marymakerstudio.com.au

MODERN MACRAMÉ

USA, international shipping
Modernmacrame.com

NIROMA STUDIO

USA, international shipping
niromastudio.com

HOW TO MEASURE CORDS FOR YOUR OWN DESIGNS

In this book, you will find all the measurements for each project, but if you want to create your own pieces, then the information below will be of help.

There is no magical formula to calculate the length of cords precisely. This is because measurements may vary according to a few different factors: the type of rope (thickness and material), whether you tend to tie the knots more tightly or loosely, the type of project, the design and the knots used in the project.

However, don't feel overwhelmed! Remember that practice makes perfect and as you make your way in the macramé world you will find a measuring technique that fits you.

Here, we share ours: We keep some past projects which we use for reference—they are all different in knots and length. Some of them have more knots, and that is what we mainly consider together with the material we use—remember that the material plays an important role and can make a difference. So, when we are working on a new project, we go back to those reference pieces and check whether we have to multiply or if that length is enough for our project.

For example, let's say we cut 8.2-foot (2.5-m)-long pieces of cord and we are able to knot 12 inches (30 cm), leaving 6 inches (15 cm) as fringe. We want the new project to be 24 inches (60 cm) long, so we will have to double the length of our reference piece, that would be 16.4 feet (5 m) long. Nevertheless, remember this is just an example, because there are some other factors that may alter the measurements.

WHAT TO DO WITH LEFTOVERS

Leftovers should never go into the trash! You can always reuse them as part of other projects. They can become beautiful feathers, tassels or you can also use them in bigger projects as fringe for wall hangings. So, always keep them in a leftovers' bag or box and you will be happy to see how you can creatively make the most of your extra cords!

WHAT TYPE ARE THE BEST DOWELS?

We live near the sea, so we constantly find pretty driftwood pieces. Even though we adore using those pieces, sometimes they are not the best option for some projects if they are not straight. Also, driftwood that has big curves may make your work a bit tedious if you are not an experienced maker. That is why we suggest you work with either natural driftwood, which is fairly straight, or industrialized wooden sticks—this will guarantee that you won't have problems.

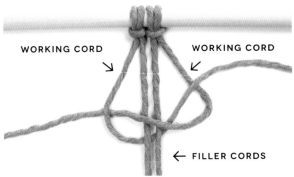

WORKING CORD ↘   WORKING CORD ↙

← FILLER CORDS

HOW TO CLEAN NATURAL DRIFTWOOD

Driftwood pieces have a unique natural beauty; however, you have to carefully clean them to get rid of sand, dirt and even worms! First, use a brush or piece of cloth to remove the visible dirt or dust. An eco-friendly way to clean the pieces thoroughly is by using baking soda and vinegar. Put the driftwood into a container and fill it with water. After that, pour a quantity of baking soda and double that quantity in vinegar. Leave the driftwood there for at least 2 hours. Rinse with fresh water and lay them out to dry. Sand the pieces to give them a final touch and enjoy using them!

TAKING CARE OF YOUR FINISHED MACRAMÉ PIECES

As you will be using 100% cotton cords, they can be hand-washed. However, for obvious reasons, it is not the best option for all pieces. You can wash a curtain, a rug, a table mat or a coaster, but for the rest of the macramé pieces, we suggest simply dusting them regularly. Tassels and fringe may tend to look a bit messy after some time, so brush them from time to time in order to keep a neat appearance. You can use any brush you have at home.

USEFUL VOCABULARY

WORKING CORDS: These are the cords in a macramé project that you are going to use to tie around filler or guiding cords. (See image above for reference.)

FILLER CORDS: These are the cords in a macramé project that will be inside the working cords. They are not used to tie.

GUIDING CORDS: These are the cords in a macramé project used as reference when tying Double Half Hitch Knots (page 21).

FRINGE: A decorative border of hanging threads left loose as part of a macramé project.

Basic Knots & Patterns

WHERE THE MAGIC BEGINS

Let us tell you a secret . . . this is not the first time you are going to tie a macramé knot. You've been doing it all throughout your life without even realizing it! You may experience a kind of throwback to your childhood, when you learned to tie your shoelaces after some trials, or when making a bow for a wrapped present. Also, if you used to make those colorful corded bracelets with your friends during the summertime, these knots will be a piece of cake for you!

When it comes to macramé, you don't need to learn a wide variety of knots in order to create outstanding pieces, and that is the essence of our work. Our hope is that you enjoy the elegance of simplicity as much as we do.

In this part, we have included a fine selection of the most basic macramé knots you MUST know for sure. They are carefully explained with step-by-step pictures that will guide you to success. These knots will also be used to create a fine variety of patterns, like diamonds, clusters and zig zags.

We all have different learning styles, and macramé is a trial-and-error art, so don't feel overwhelmed if you don't get the knots at first—it also took us some practice until we could manage them. That is why we strongly advise you practice each knot on its own (apart from your project) as many times as you need before moving ahead in your project.

And now, grab some cords . . . macramé is waiting for you!

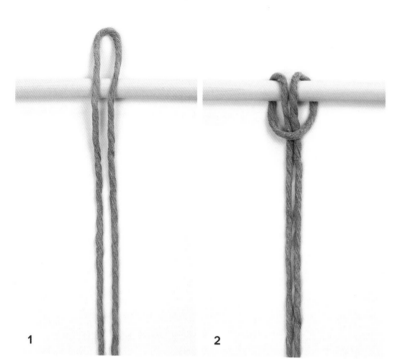

THE KNOTS

LARK'S HEAD KNOT

This is the most basic knot used to start working on your macramé pieces; usually we use this knot to tie the cords to the dowel. It is also used to attach cord to another piece of cord, for example, to add fringe.

1. Take the working cord and fold it in half. Place the loop over the dowel.

2. Keep the 2 ends in your hands and place them inside the loop. Rotate the loop slightly to the back of the dowel.

3. Pull the cords tight.

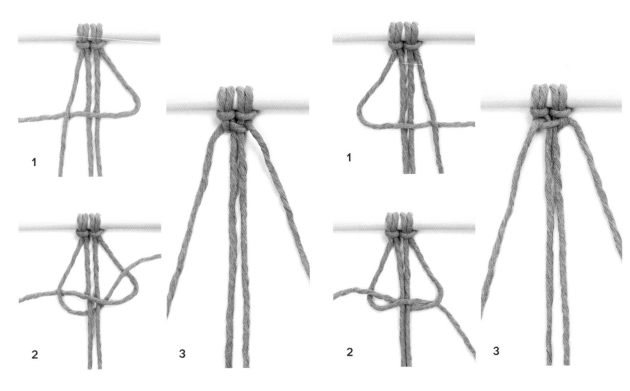

HALF KNOT (RIGHT FACING)

For this knot, you will always need an even number of cords to work with. To set up for a Half Knot, tie 2 pieces of cord to a dowel using the Lark's Head Knot (page 16). Its most common use is to make a Half Knot Sinnet (page 24).

1. Take the right outer cord and place it over the 2 inner cords and under the left outer cord.

2. Take the left outer cord and bring it under the 2 filler cords. Take it outside the loop formed on the previous step, over the right outer cord.

3. Pull the cords tight.

HALF KNOT (LEFT FACING)

1. Take the outer left cord and place it over the 2 inner cords and under the right outer cord.

2. Take the right outer cord and bring it under the 2 filler cords. Take it outside the loop formed on the previous step, over the left outer cord.

3. Pull the cords tight.

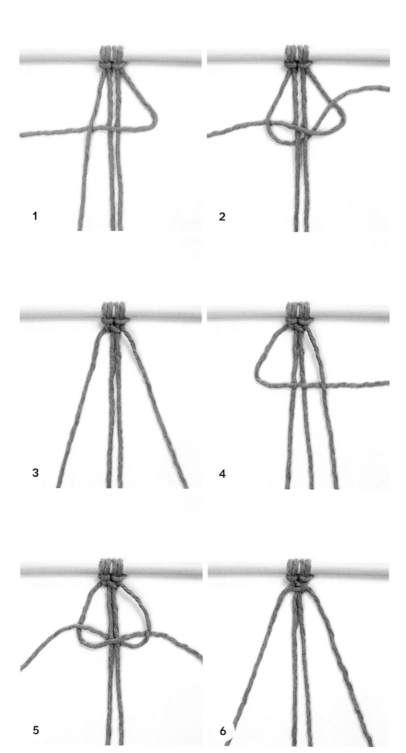

SQUARE KNOT (RIGHT FACING)

This knot is a combination of a Right Facing Half Knot and Left Facing Half Knot. You can start it on the side you prefer but doing it always to the same side makes the pattern look more organic and neater. You will need an even set of cords to start working. For each Square Knot, you need 4 cords.

1. Use 4 cords. Take the right outer cord and place it over the 2 inner cords and under the left outer cord.

2. Take the left outer cord and bring it under the 2 filler cords. Take it outside the loop formed on the previous step, over the right outer cord.

3. Pull the cords tight.

4. Take the left outer cord and place it over the 2 inner cords and under the right outer cord.

5. Take the right outer cord and bring it under the 2 filler cords. Take it outside the loop formed on the previous step, over the left outer cord.

6. Pull the cords tight.

SQUARE KNOT (LEFT FACING)

Remember you can start the knot to whatever side you prefer, so this time we will only change the side and start leftwards.

1. Take the left outer cord and place it over the 2 inner cords and under the outer right cord.

2. Take the right outer cord and bring it under the 2 filler cords. Take it outside the loop formed on the previous step, over the left outer cord.

3. Pull the cords tight.

4. Take the right outer cord and place it over the 2 inner cords and under the left outer cord.

5. Take the left outer cord and bring it under the 2 filler cords. Take it outside the loop formed on the previous step, over the right outer cord.

6. Pull the cords tight.

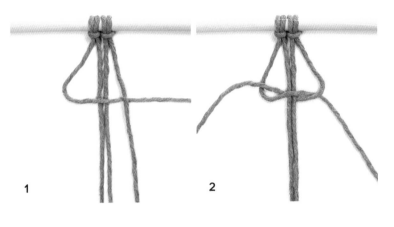

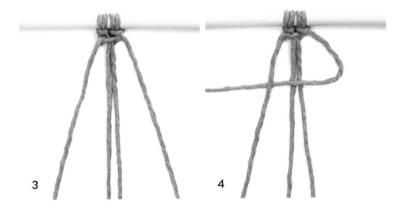

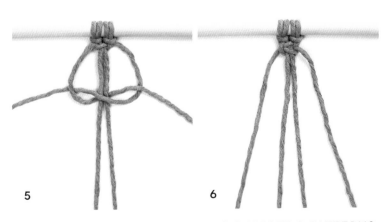

1

SQUARE KNOT WITH MULTIPLE FILLER CORDS

In order to add more texture to a design you can make bigger Square Knots. To achieve this, use 4 or more filler cords.

1. In order to make this knot, you need to have 6 cords total, or more. Take the 2 outer cords as the working cords and leave all the rest of the cords as filler cords. Refer to the Square Knot (either right facing or left facing) on pages 18 or 19. In order to make the design look neater, avoid overlapping the inner cords.

DOUBLE HALF HITCH KNOT

This knot is elegant and versatile and will allow you to create a wide variety of patterns, whether you do it vertically or horizontally/diagonally. We use it a lot all throughout the designs and you will end up loving it.

To start, you need a reference cord as a guide. Remember that guiding cords are the ones used to shape the direction when tying Double Half Hitch Knots.

DOUBLE HALF HITCH KNOT: VERTICAL

1. Take the left cord as a guide and place it over the working cord.

2. Tie the working cord around the guiding cord forming a loop and pass it through the space between the working and the guiding cords.

3. Pull the cords tight. Up to here, you have done a simple Half Hitch Knot.

4. Repeat the procedure using the same working cord (which is on the left now). The 2nd knot is the one that secures and ends the Double Half Hitch Knot.

NOTE: If you want to make the knot on the other side, start step 1 by taking the right cord as the guide.

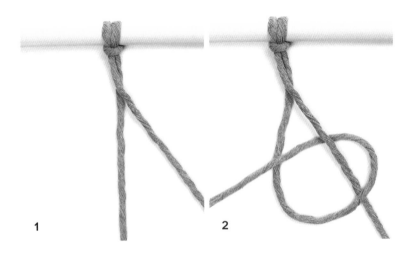

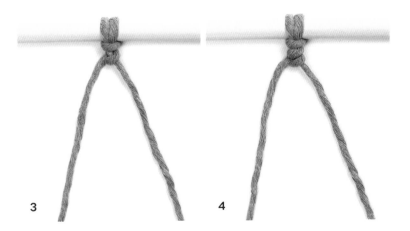

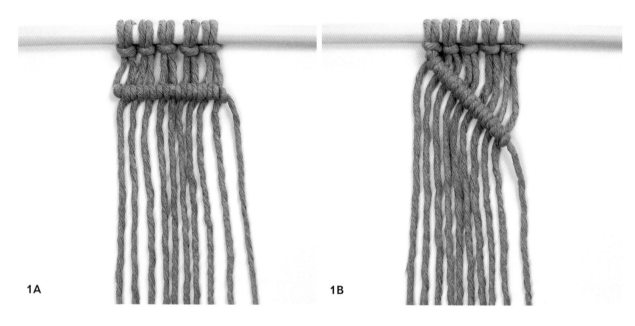

1A

1B

DOUBLE HALF HITCH KNOT: HORIZONTAL/DIAGONAL

1. Take the outer cord as a guide (or an extra cord if specified) and place it over the rest of the cords you are going to tie. Keep it either horizontal or diagonal, depending on the design you want to create. The working cord we are going to use is the one immediately after the guiding cord. Refer to the Double Half Hitch Knot (page 21) and tie a sequence of Double Half Hitches until you reach the desired length.

TIP: In order to prevent warping when knotting a long sequence of Double Half Hitch Knots, we suggest you do the following: Start knotting a Double Half Hitch Knot as described, but then continue knotting while alternating between a Double Half Hitch Knot and a simple Half Hitch Knot. Refer to the Double Half Hitch Knot on page 21 and follow the steps until step 3 for a simple Half Hitch Knot.

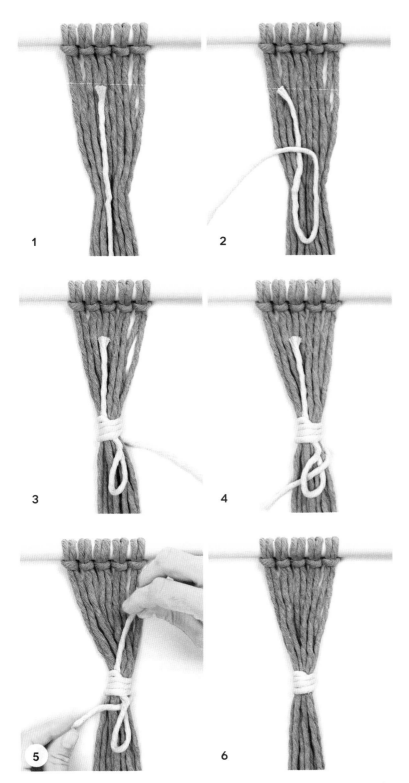

GATHERING KNOT

As its name suggests, this knot is used to gather a set of cords together and to tie them tightly. Even though we mainly use it to start and finish plant hangers, you will also find it in other projects. It is usually used to give final touches to a piece or when making tassels or joining the different parts of a project.

1. Gather all the cords you want to tie together. Take an extra cord and place it over the gathered cords.

2. Make a loop at the bottom by folding the extra cord. Leave a short tail of the cord on the top.

3. Use the longer end of the extra cord to wrap the cords downwards.

4. Once you reach the loop, pass the cord through it.

5. Take both ends of the extra cord and pull them tight. Pull the top end of the cord again so that it hides inside the wrapping.

6. Cut both ends of the extra cord close to the gathering knot.

1

2

THE PATTERNS

HALF KNOT SINNET

You have surely seen this pattern before since it is one of the most commonly known macramé patterns for plant hangers. It is ideal for giving texture to your designs and accents every macramé piece.

If you choose to make all left facing Half Knots you will create a right-twisting sinnet (like in the example image above). On the contrary, if you choose to make all right facing Half Knots, you will create a left-twisting sinnet.

1. Tie 2 pieces of cord to a dowel, a ring or to another piece of cord using the Lark's Head Knot. When forming the Lark's Head Knot, fold the cords so that the 2 inner cords are shorter than the outer ones.

Mind that the inner cords are just filler cords; the outer cords should be longer since they are the working cords.

2. Start knotting the Half Knot (either right facing or left facing) as described on page 17. Repeat the same knot sequence until you reach the desired length. Avoid leaving gaps in between the knots by tying each knot tightly to each other.

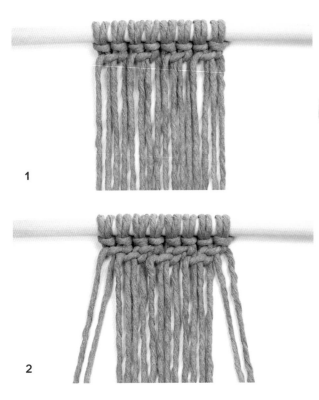

1

2

3

ALTERNATING HALF KNOT

You can create a nice and simple pattern by alternating Half Knots. We prefer how this pattern looks when knotting Half Knots always to the same side (shown in the images above), though you can alternate between left-facing and right-facing Half Knots. This versatility gives you the freedom to play and be creative when designing your own projects.

1. Refer to the Half Knot on page 17 and tie a 1st row of Half Knots.

2. For the following row, leave the first 2 and the last 2 cords without knotting. Tie another row of Half Knots.

3. Continue knotting, repeating step 1 and 2 until you get the desired length of the pattern.

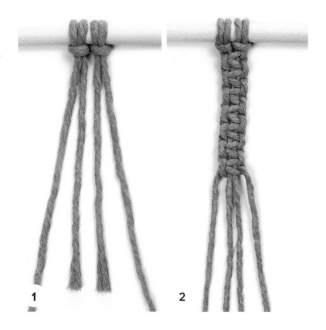

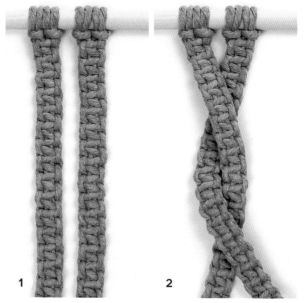

SQUARE KNOT SINNET

Sinnets are perfect for plant hangers, but they definitely highlight other designs too. There is a wide variety of patterns you can make by combining and braiding them.

1. Tie 2 pieces of cord using the Lark's Head Knot. When forming the Lark's Head Knot, fold the cords so that the 2 inner cords are shorter than the outer ones. Mind that the inner cords are just filler cords, so the outer cords should be longer since they are the working cords.

2. Start knotting Square Knots (see page 18). Mind that you should always start tying to the same side. Continue until you reach the desired length. Avoid leaving gaps in between the knots by tying each knot tightly to each other.

SQUARE KNOT BRAID WITH 2 SINNETS

Braids add beauty and texture to your designs. With this pattern, you can make a simple braid using 2 Square Knot Sinnets.

1. Make 2 Square Knot Sinnets, one next to the other, leaving a space of approximately 4 inches (10 cm).

2. Braid the 2 Square Knots Sinnets, crossing them up to the end. Braids can come undone easily, so at this point, we suggest working on a flat surface to avoid this. Finish braids by tying them off with a Gathering Knot (see page 23).

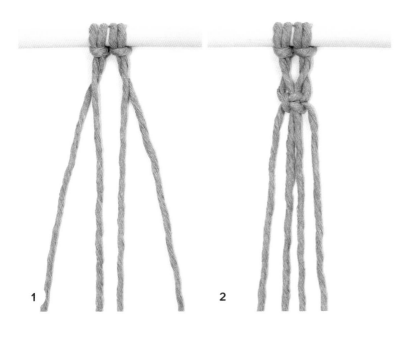

SQUARE KNOT SINNET ALTERNATING INNER & OUTER CORDS

This variation of the Square Knot Sinnet is a clear example of how easily you can change the look of a knot. It is as simple as alternating the position of the working cords.

1. Tie 2 pieces of cord to a dowel, a ring or to another piece of cord using the Lark's Head Knot on page 16. Now, we are going to alternate the filler and working cords. Take the 2 inner cords, bring them to the outside (under the other cords) and use them as working cords.

2. Refer to page 18 and tie a Square Knot using the 2 new working cords. In order to make this knot noticeable, it is necessary to leave a considerable space between each square knot.

3. Keep on knotting a sequence of Square Knots, alternating the inner and outer cords until you reach the desired length.

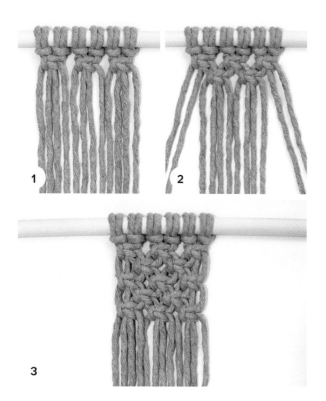

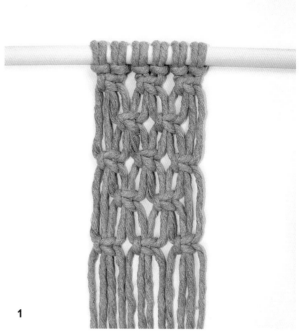

ALTERNATING SQUARE KNOT

Alternating Square Knots is the most commonly used pattern in macramé. It is plain and delicate, which makes it ideal for beginners. Following this tutorial are also some variations on this pattern, to show you all kinds of simple ways you can get creative new looks in your macramé art!

1. Refer to the Square Knot on page 18 and tie a 1st row of Square Knots.

2. For the 2nd row, leave the first 2 and the last 2 cords without knotting. Tie another row of Square Knots.

3. Continue knotting, repeating steps 1 and 2, until you get the desired length of the pattern.

LOOSE ALTERNATING SQUARE KNOT

1. Refer to the Alternating Square Knot. Leave a considerable space between each row of Square Knots you tie.

TIP: The look of Alternating Square Knots may vary according to the space you leave between each row. Be consistent with the space you leave in order to get a neat design.

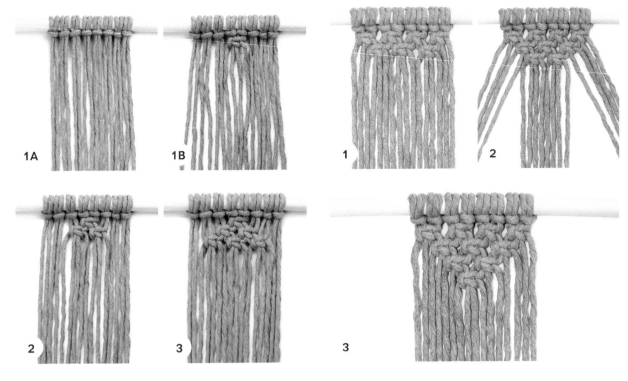

INCREASING ALTERNATING SQUARE KNOT

1. For this pattern, you need an even set of cords. Take the 4 cords in the middle and tie a Square Knot.

2. For the following row, take 2 cords from the previous Square Knot and use them to tie a Square Knot using the 2 cords immediately next to it. Do the same to the other side. You will get a row of 2 Square Knots.

3. For the following rows, start always from the outer part of the design, adding 2 cords at the beginning and at the end of each row.

DECREASING ALTERNATING SQUARE KNOT

1. For this pattern, you need an even set of cords. Tie 2 rows of Alternating Square Knots.

2. For the 3rd row of Square Knots, leave the first 4 and the last 4 cords without knotting and tie Square Knots using the remaining cords.

3. Keep on leaving 2 more cords without knotting for each row of Square Knots you start until you only have 4 cords to tie.

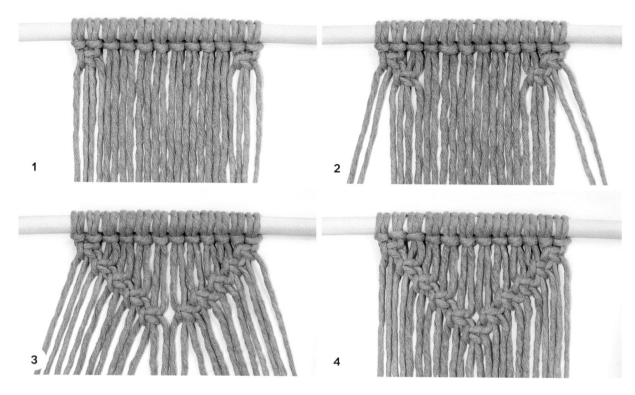

SQUARE KNOTS V-SHAPE

1. For this pattern, you need an even set of cords. For the 1st row use the first 4 and the last 4 cords and tie a Square Knot (page 18) on each set of cords.

2. In the 2nd row, leave the first 2 and the last 2 cords of the Square Knots without tying. Take the next 2 cords to make a set of 4 cords and tie a Square Knot.

3. Keep on knotting Square Knots diagonally, leaving 2 more cords without tying for each row of Square Knots you start until you only have 4 cords to tie.

4. Finish the pattern with a Square Knot.

TIP: If you keep on knotting a continuous horizontal sequence of this pattern you will get a lovely zig-zag pattern. We particularly love it and use it a lot.

1

2

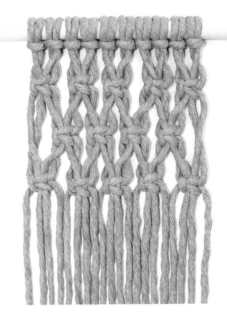

3

SQUARE KNOT ALTERNATING INNER & OUTER CORDS (SWITCH SQUARE KNOT)

This subtle variation for the Alternating Square Knot pattern creates a completely different look. It is a simple way to vary and highlight your designs.

1. Refer to the pattern for the Square Knot Sinnet Alternating Inner and Outer Cords on page 27. Tie a row of Square Knots, keeping the pattern loose and alternating the inner and outer cords.

2. For the following row, leave the first 2 and the last 2 cords without tying and tie another row of Square Knots, alternating the inner and outer cords.

3. In the next row, start tying using all the cords and keeping the alternating inner and outer cords design. Continue knotting, repeating steps 1 and 2 until you get the desired length of the pattern.

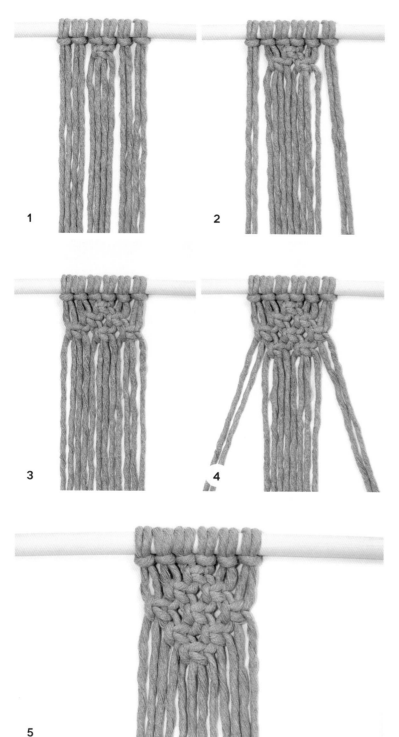

1

2

3

4

5

SQUARE KNOT CLUSTERS (BIG & SMALL)

These are fun patterns you can add everywhere in your projects. Here we are going to show how to make these patterns in two different sizes, big and small diamonds. In order to create this pattern, you will have to increase and decrease alternating square knots.

BIG CLUSTER

1. For the big pattern, you need a minimum of 12 cords. Start using the 4 cords in the middle and tie a Square Knot (page 18).

2. For the 2nd row, leave the first 2 and the last 2 cords without knotting and tie 2 Square Knots.

3. Start the 3rd row using all the cords and tie 3 Square Knots. What you have done up to here is an increasing Square Knot pattern.

4. From now on, you will make a decreasing Square Knot pattern. Leave the 2 first and the 2 last cords without knotting and make 2 Square Knots.

5. Finish the pattern making a Square Knot using the 4 cords in the middle.

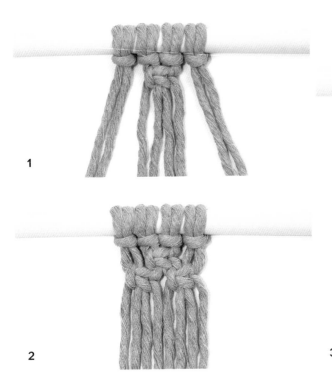

SMALL CLUSTER

1. For the small pattern, you need a minimum of 8 cords. Start using the 4 cords in the middle and tie a Square Knot (page 18).

2. Start the 2nd row using all the cords and tie 2 Square Knots.

3. Finish the pattern making a Square Knot using the 4 cords in the middle.

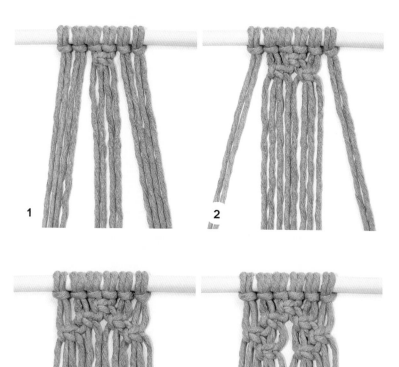

DIAMOND PATTERNS

If you are into macramé, you may have certainly noticed that diamonds are by far makers' favorite patterns. And that is because they allow you to play with texture, size and a variety of designs inside them. Even if you make just one diamond in your design or if you make an entire design using only diamonds, you will get a stunning piece without any doubt.

SQUARE KNOT DIAMOND

1. For this pattern, you need an even set of cords. Start using the 4 cords in the middle and tie a Square Knot (page 18).

2. In the 2nd row, leave the first 2 and the last 2 cords without knotting and tie 2 Square Knots.

3. Take only the first 4 and the last 4 outer cords and tie 2 Square Knots.

4. Now, you will start decreasing Square Knots diagonally. Leave the first 2 and the last 2 cords without knotting and tie 2 Square Knots.

5. Finish the pattern making a Square Knot using the 4 cords in the middle.

DOUBLE HALF HITCH KNOT DIAMOND

1. Take the 2 cords in the middle. Use one of them as the guiding cord and the other one as the working cord. Tie a simple Half Hitch Knot (page 17). This is the top of the diamond.

2. Now, use the 2 cords on step 1 as guiding cords, one for the left side and one for the right side of the diamond. Use the working cords on the left and on the right to tie Double Half Hitches (page 22) diagonally around both guiding cords until you reach the desired length.

3. Continue using the same guiding cords, but now position them diagonally to the center in order to make the diamond shape.

4. Tie Double Half Hitches around both guiding cords until the guiding cords meet in the middle. Finish the diamond using the guiding cords to tie a Double Half Hitch Knot. This is the bottom of the diamond.

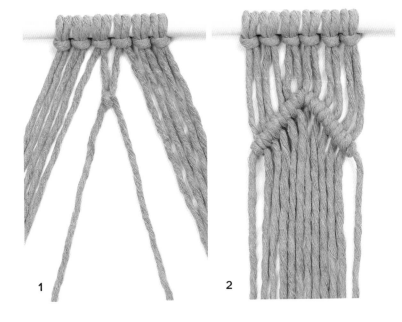

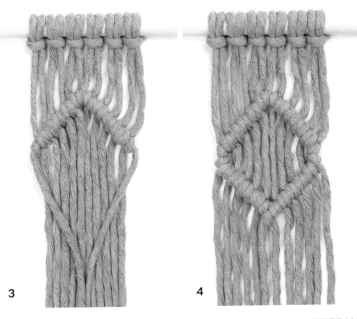

DOUBLE-DOUBLE HALF HITCH KNOT DIAMOND

1. Refer to the Double Half Hitch Knot Diamond pattern explained before on page 35 and follow the procedure until step 3. Then, take again the 2 cords in the middle and tie a simple Half Hitch Knot (page 17).

2. Use those cords as guiding cords to tie Double Half Hitches (page 22) diagonally around both guiding cords until you complete the design. Make sure you place the guiding cords close to the previous row.

3. Continue using the same guiding cords, but now position them diagonally to the center in order to make the diamond shape. Tie Double Half Hitches around both guiding cords until the guiding cords meet in the middle. Take the 2 outer cords and use them as guiding cords to tie another row of Double Half Hitches.

4. Finish the diamond using the guiding cords to tie a Double Half Hitch Knot (page 21). This is the bottom of the double diamond.

1

2

PATTERNS INSIDE A DIAMOND

Diamonds have their own beauty, but you can accent them and make them even more spectacular by adding different patterns inside them.

Start the diamond as explained; it may be a Double Half Hitch Diamond (page 35) or a Square Knot Diamond (page 34). Then, choose from the patterns in this book and tie them in the center of the diamond. Finish the diamond.

YOU CAN USE PATTERNS LIKE:

Square Knot with Multiple Filler Cords, page 20 (image 1 at left)
Square Knot Clusters, page 32 (image 2 at left)
Square Knot, page 18 (image 3 at left)

3

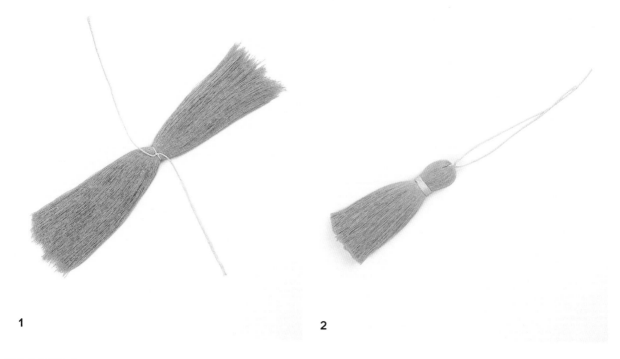

1   2

TASSELS

Tassels are without any doubt a charming and soft detail to add to your projects! Whether you use only one tassel or if they are the stars of the piece, they will definitely highlight the beauty of your project. Let's see how to make and add them!

MAKING TASSELS

In order to make tassels, you will need at least 2 pieces of 12mm single-twist cotton string and 2 pieces of a thin cord.

1. Take the 2 pieces of 12mm single-twist cotton string and brush them until they are completely unraveled. Use a piece of a thin and strong cotton cord to tie them in the middle. Bear in mind that this cord is the one that will be used to attach the tassel to the macramé piece, so it must have a considerable length; 10 inches (25 cm) would work well.

2. Take the ends of the thin cord and fold the brushed cords in half. Use another piece of the thin cotton cord, a longer one (12 inches [30 cm] would work well) and tie the tassel with a Gathering Knot (page 23). Trim the ends and brush it again.

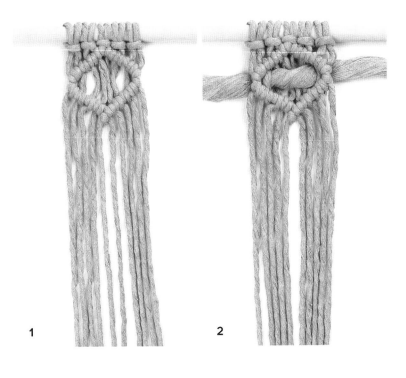

MAKING A TASSEL WITHIN A DIAMOND PATTERN

1. In order to be able to add a tassel to a piece you need a diamond to place it inside. Take the cords in the middle of the diamond in order to open two spaces where you will pass the cord.

2. Take a piece of 12mm single-twist cotton string and pass each end through the holes you have just opened in the diamond. Both ends will be now at the back of the diamond.

3. Use your fingers to open a hole in the middle of the diamond and pass both ends of the 12mm cord through that hole to bring them to the front part of the diamond.

4. Brush the tassel and trim the ends.

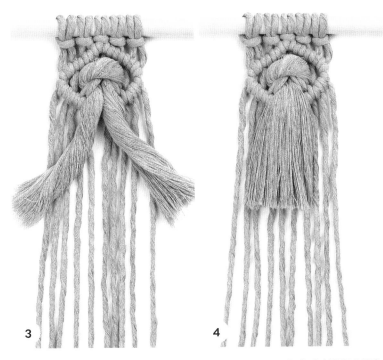

NOTE: If you don't have 12mm cotton cord, you can also make the tassels by gathering many pieces of a thinner cord. It will take longer to brush them, but it works well too!

A BLANK CANVAS

SIMPLE PROJECTS
FOR GUARANTEED SUCCESS

Every time an artist faces a blank canvas, amazing things can happen. It is a moment of imagination and creativity, of brain-heart-hands connection in which everything flows to make magic happen. Inspiration may be everywhere, so be ready to explore the world around you and let yourself be surprised with the beauty you will be able to create!

We vividly remember our feelings when we met those long cords hanging from a wooden dowel for the first time! After practicing the basic knots, we knew that the time had come to move a step forward. Even though we felt really tempted to start with a big and ambitious piece on our own, we knew that a guided project was more appropriate for us in order to have a good start.

The main aim of this section is to let you have a first exciting encounter with macramé, in a way that you enjoy. We have designed these four projects for you, not only because they are simple and easy to follow, but also because you are going to make them in a matter of minutes! Of course, the more you practice, the quicker you will to be able to make them. And that is what makes macramé so fascinating!

After you make one (or more) of the pieces in this section, you can be fully confident choosing from any of the other projects in this book, knowing that you will be capable of doing them successfully. You are already familiar with the basic knots, so now the time has come for you to put your hands into action! Have fun and enjoy it!

Classic Plant Hanger

3.3 feet (1 m) long

MATERIALS

Wooden ring, 3 inches (7 cm) diameter

3mm 3-strand twisted cotton cord, about 83 feet (25.4 m) total

CUTS

8 pieces, 118 inches (300 cm) long

2 pieces, 27.5 inches (70 cm) long

KNOTS & PATTERNS

Gathering Knot (page 23)

Half Knot Sinnet (page 24)

Square Knot (page 18)

When thinking about macramé, one of the things that probably first comes to your mind are plant hangers. This is mainly because they were really popular during the '70s, and now they have come back in style as a beautiful way to highlight the natural beauty of plants.

Simple and easy to do but delicate and sophisticated, this plant hanger is a great opportunity to tackle the knots you've already learned and achieve an amazing result in a couple of minutes. We hope you enjoy the process!

1. Hang a wooden ring; it could be from a hook, for example. Take the 8 cords and pass them through the wooden ring. Fold each one over the ring so that one part is 79 inches (200 cm) long and the other part is 39.5 inches (100 cm) long. Shorter cords will work as the inner filler cords and longer cords will work as the outer working cords. Use a piece 27.5 inches (70 cm) long to tie a Gathering Knot close to the ring.

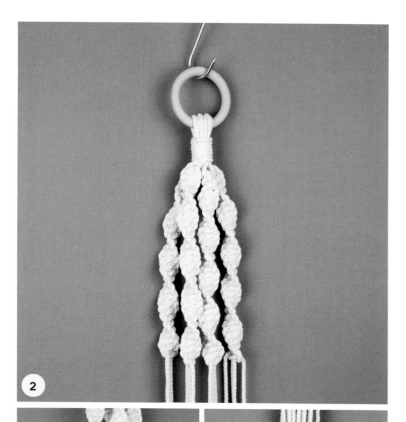

2. Take 2 long cords as the outer working cords and 2 short cords as the inner filler cords and make a Half Knot Sinnet. Tie the Half Knots until the outer cords reach the length of the inner cords (30 knots approximately). Repeat the same procedure until you get 4 Half Knot Sinnets.

3. Take 2 cords from one of the Half Knot Sinnets and 2 cords from the Half Knot Sinnet immediately next to it and tie a Square Knot leaving a space of 9 inches (23 cm) from the sinnets. Repeat this step using the remaining cords until all the sinnets are connected.

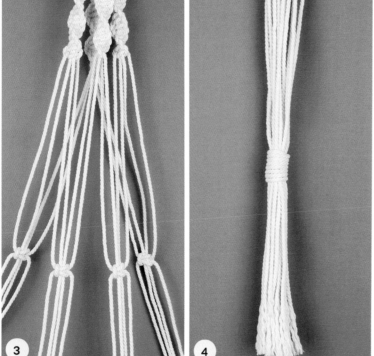

4. Use a piece of 27.5 inch (70 cm) cord to finish the hanger with a Gathering Knot. Leave a space of 6 inches (15 cm) between the Square Knots and the Gathering Knot. Trim the ends and unravel them.

You can hang your plant hanger from the ceiling using an open eye bolt or hang it on the walls using brackets.

Textured coaster

Coasters are by far our favorite project for beginners! They are small pieces that you will be able to produce in a few minutes—that gives you the opportunity to practice a lot. We think they are a great option when making handmade presents too! Besides, you can choose from a wide range of knots and patterns to create your own designs and make them look stylish. This pretty design with only two basic knots will make your table look really cool! Let's go for it!

FINISHED SIZE

9 inches long x 5 inches wide (22 cm long x 12 cm wide)

MATERIALS

Wooden dowel, at least 8 inches (20 cm) long (only needed to knot the design, then taken off)

5mm single-twist cotton string, about 36 feet (11 m) total

CUTS

10 pieces, 43.5 inches (110 cm) long

KNOTS & PATTERNS

Lark's Head Knot (page 16)

Alternating Square Knot (page 28)

Alternating Half Knot (page 25)

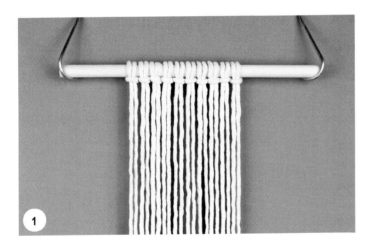

1. Tie all the pieces to the dowel using the Lark's Head Knot. You will only need to use the dowel to hang the design while knotting; once it is finished, you'll take the macramé off of the dowel.

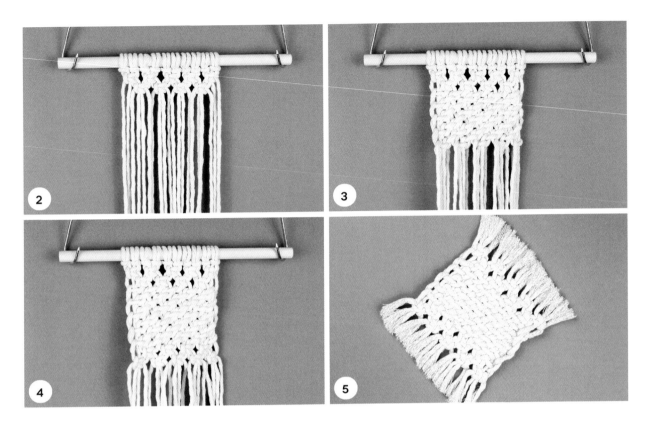

2. Tie 2 rows of Alternating Square Knots. Try to tie them tight so that the knots don't come undone.

3. Tie 9 rows of Alternating Half Knots. Don't forget to be consistent with how tight you tie the knots so that the pattern looks neat.

4. Tie 2 rows of Alternating Square Knots again. Start the 1st row of Square Knots, leaving the first 2 cords without knotting so that the 2nd final row is complete and the design is consistent.

5. Take the coaster off the dowel and trim the ends so that they all have the same length and brush them.

DELicate GARLand

When it comes to a kid's bedroom, playroom or any room with whimsical décor, garlands are a nice way of including some macramé. We really like how cute they look both on the walls and on furniture like shelves or a baby cradle. They are also perfect for party decorations, don't you think?

This project is fun and approachable for beginners since you are going to produce the same pattern many times until you finish the whole design of the garland. Try to be consistent with how tight you tie since the garland should look uniform and clean.

FINISHED SIZE
3.3 feet (1 m) long

MATERIALS
5mm single-twist cotton string, about 36 feet (11 m) total

High-quality Scotch or masking tape

CUTS
10 pieces, 35.5 inches (90 cm) long

1 piece, 79 inches (200 cm) long

KNOTS & PATTERNS
Lark's Head Knot (page 16)

Square Knot V-shape (page 30)

Diagonal Double Half Hitch Knot (page 22)

1. To start this project, first attach the 79-inch (200-cm)-long cord on a table or onto another flat horizontal surface; we recommend using high-quality tape. Leave an end of 20 inches (50 cm) and tie the 10 pieces of 35.5 inch (90 cm) cord from it using the Lark's Head Knot.

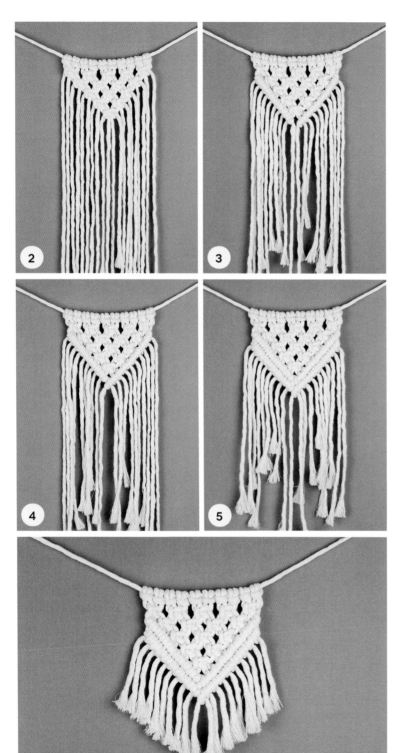

2. Use all the cords to tie a Square Knot V-shape until you have 4 cords to tie the last Square Knot.

3. Take the outer cords from both sides and make a 1st row of Diagonal Double Half Hitches.

4. Tie the ends in the middle with a Double Half Hitch Knot.

5. Repeat step 3 to make another row of Diagonal Double Half Hitches. Tie the ends in the middle as in step 4.

6. Trim the ends, making a V-shape, and brush them.

Repeat this procedure to make 5 more buntings. Leave a 2-inch (5-cm) space between each of them. Hang it and enjoy!

Timeless Wall Hanging

Have you ever pictured yourself making a macramé wall hanging? Crazy, isn't it? Those stunning and eye-catching pieces of art that you see on the internet or in home décor shops are now at your fingertips.

Allow yourself to have fun during this process and be ready to have all your friends asking you for a wall hanging after making this one! We think this design is perfectly suitable if you are new to macramé because with only two knots, you will create an elegant piece which will add a modern accent to your home. And beyond that, you will experience the reward of creating a handmade piece of art.

FINISHED SIZE

24 inches long x 10 inches wide (60 cm long x 26 cm wide)

MATERIALS

Wooden dowel, 12 inches (30 cm) long

5mm single-twist cotton string, about 173 feet (52.6 m) total

CUTS

8 pieces, 87 inches (220 cm) long

14 pieces, 98 inches (250 cm) long

KNOTS & PATTERNS

Lark's Head Knot (page 16)

Decreasing Alternating Square Knot (page 29)

Square Knot Small Cluster (page 33)

V-shape of Square Knots (page 30)

Diagonal Double Half Hitch Knot (page 22)

1. Attach 4 of the 87-inch (220-cm)-long cords onto the dowel with the Lark's Head Knot. Continue attaching all 14 of the 98-inch (250-cm)-long cords and then the remaining 87-inch (220-cm)-long cords.

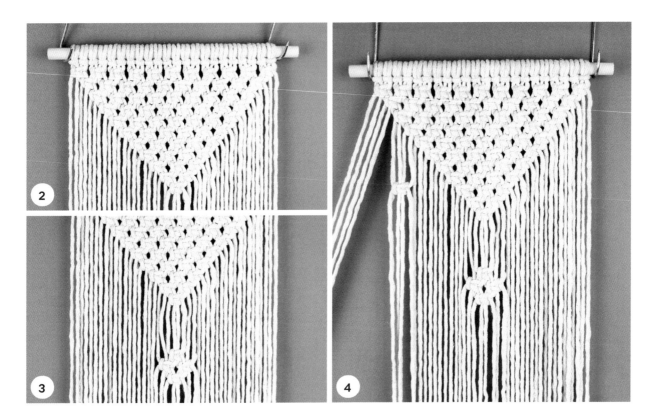

2. Use all the cords to tie a Decreasing Alternating Square Knot pattern.

3. Leave a space of 2 inches (5 cm) from the Decreasing Alternating Square Knots pattern and take the 4 cords in the middle of the piece to tie a Square Knot Small Cluster pattern.

4. In order to make another Square Knot Small Cluster on the left, leave the first 4 outer cords without tying and tie a Square Knot leaving 2 inches (5 cm) from the Decreasing Alternating Square Knot pattern.

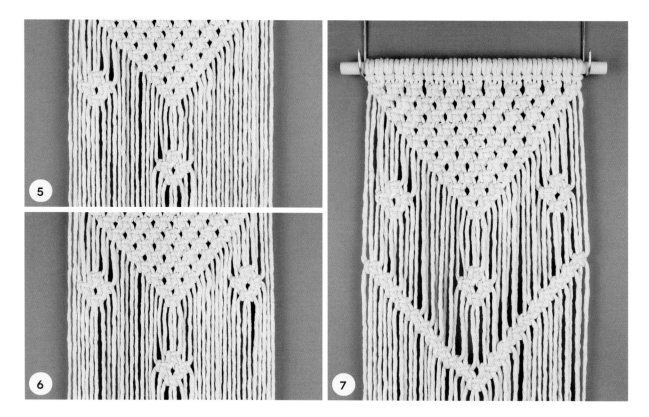

5. Complete the Square Knot Small Cluster.

6. Make a Square Knot Small Cluster on the right by repeating steps 4 and 5.

7. Leave 2 inches (5 cm) from the outer clusters and tie a V-shape of Square Knots.

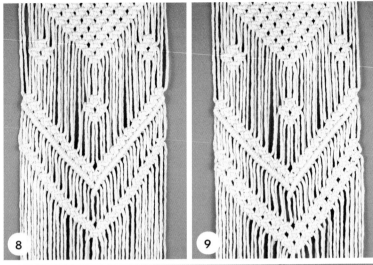

8. Use the outer cords as guides and make a Diagonal Double Half Hitch pattern close to the V-shape of Square Knots. Leave 2 inches (5 cm) from the outer parts of the Diagonal Double Half Hitches and tie a V-shape of Square Knots.

9. Tie another V-shape of Square Knots close to the previous one.

10. Trim and slightly brush the ends.

Let's Rock It

BIGGER PROJECTS FOR HOME DÉCOR

The number of macramé fans around the world grows every day and we think this is due to the fact that macramé is not only a beautiful technique, but also a versatile one. It is amazing to see the innumerable projects you can make, from decorating the floor to ceilings and walls!

Now that you are familiar with the basic knots and have practiced a project or two from the previous section, you can jump into any of these projects with the conviction that you'll get great results! We are sure you will find a lot of satisfaction creating simple but stunning pieces for your home or any special place.

Knots will start flowing gently through your hands and without even noticing it, you'll end up mastering this art!

At first glance, big projects may seem a bit intimidating, but believe us that you have already learned all the necessary knots and tips to tackle them without any problems! You'll find yourself admiring your creations and your abilities and, what's more, you'll be as proud of yourself as we already are!

on the walls

There are an endless number of things you can use to dress a wall, from paintings and mirrors, to pictures, clocks and shelves. But it can't be denied that macramé is one of the most popular arts today to adds an accent piece to any room.

Wall hangings are the stars of macramé art, but there is a wide variety of other macramé pieces you can create to include as wall décor. In this part of the book, you will find an interesting collection of different projects for wall art, such as a charming mirror (page 91), a delicate and cute shelf (page 97) and, of course, a selection of some amazing wall hangings (pages 61, 65, 69, 77, 83 and 87) that will definitely delight your eyes.

Don't hesitate to choose any one of these projects. Dive right in to enjoy the process of knotting and decorating!

BaLi WaLL Hanging

Stunning and large doesn't necessarily mean intricate or difficult, and you will learn this lesson perfectly with this piece! The clear, neat lines and symmetry of a triptych like the Bali Wall Hanging is the perfect example of a stylish and simple piece. While making this wall hanging, you'll experience how amazing it feels to create an eye-catching piece of art with a very fine design. Find a nice place to hang it at home because it will be ready in a wink!

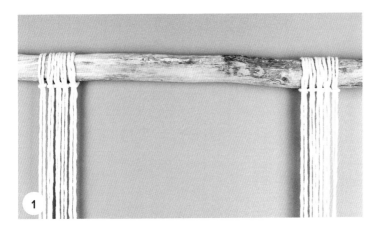

1. Attach 10 pieces of the 118-inch (300-cm)-long cords onto the wooden dowel with the Lark's Head Knot at approximately 12 inches (30 cm) from the outer parts of the dowel. Attach 5 pieces on the left and 5 pieces on the right.

FINISHED SIZE
3.3 feet wide x 34 inches long (1 m wide x 86 cm long)

MATERIALS
Wooden dowel, 3.3 feet (1 m) long

5mm single-twist cotton string, about 565 feet (172 m) total

12mm single-twist cotton string, about 24 inches (60 cm) total

48 wooden beads, 20mm diameter

High-quality Scotch or masking tape

1.5mm cotton string, about 87 inches (220 cm)

CUTS
26 pieces of 5mm single-twist cotton string, 118 inches (300 cm) long

104 pieces of 5mm single-twist cotton string, 36 inches (90 cm) long, for the fringe

2 pieces of 12mm single-twist cotton string, 12 inches (30 cm) long, for the tassel

2 pieces of 1.5mm cotton string, 12 inches (30 cm) long

2 pieces of 1.5mm cotton string, 43 inches (110 cm) long

KNOTS & PATTERNS
Lark's Head Knot (page 16)

Diagonal Double Half Hitch Knot (page 22)

Double Half Hitch Knot (page 21)

Tassel (page 38)

2. Take the outer cords from the set of cords on the left and tie 2 rows of Diagonal Double Half Hitches from left to right. Continue using the same guiding cord and tie 2 more rows of Diagonal Double Half Hitches, but this time place the guiding cord diagonally from the right to the left in order to form a zig-zag pattern. Keep on tying this pattern 4 times more. Make sure the last Diagonal Double Half Hitch row goes from the left to the right in order to be able to join it with the right side.

Repeat this procedure on the right side of the dowel but this time start and finish from the right to the left.

3. Tie one more row of Diagonal Double Half Hitches on each side and join both parts in a V-shape. Take the 2 inner cords from each part and finish the design with a Double Half Hitch Knot.

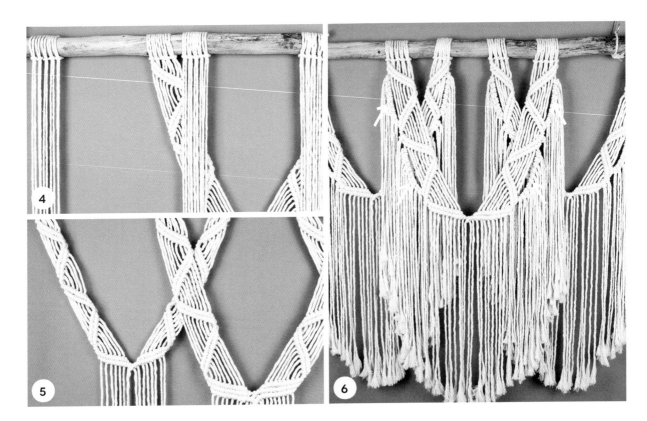

4. Attach 4 more pieces of the 118-inch (300-cm)-long cord onto the left side of the wooden dowel with the Lark's Head Knot inside the V-shape you have just tied, approximately 2.5 inches (6 cm) from it. At this point, work placing the cords over the V-shape in the middle, but once you finish the pattern place it underneath the V-shape. This will make your work easier.

Attach the other 4 pieces on the left side of the dowel at approximately 2.5 inches (6 cm) from the outer part of it. Repeat the same procedure to hang the other 8 pieces of the 118-inch (300-cm)-long cord onto the right side of the dowel.

5. This is a triptych design so you will have to make the same pattern 3 times. Repeat steps 2 and 3 using the 8 pieces of cord on the left, and again using the 8 pieces of cord on the right.

6. Use the Lark's Head Knot to add fringe to the outer edges. Tie the 36-inch (90-cm) cords in each space.

7. Attach the 2 pieces of 43-inch (110-cm)-long cord inside the 2 outer V-shapes of the design with the Lark's Head Knot. Attach 1 on the left of the V-shape and 1 on the right. Put tape on the ends of the cotton cords and pass 24 wooden beads through the cord on the left and 24 through the one on the right. Then join both sides in the middle with a Double Half Hitch Knot.

8. Use the 2 pieces of 12mm single-twist cotton string (12 inches [30 cm] long) and the 2 pieces of 1.5mm cotton string (12 inches [30 cm] long) to make a tassel. Attach it where the wooden beads join, using the cords on top of it. Congrats! You've done it! This big guy is ready to hang!

pampa wall Hanging

FINISHED SIZE
22 inches long x 12 inches wide
(55 cm long x 30 cm wide)

MATERIALS
Wooden dowel, 16 inches
(40 cm) long

5mm single-twist cotton string,
about 197 feet (60 m) total

12mm single-twist cotton
string, about 83 inches (210 cm)
total

1.5mm cotton string, about
152 inches (385 cm) total

Tapestry needle

CUTS
24 pieces of 5mm single-twist
cotton string, about 98 inches
(250 cm) long

7 pieces of 12mm single-twist
cotton string, about 12 inches
(30 cm) long, for the tassels

7 pieces of 1.5mm cotton
string, about 10 inches (25 cm)
long

7 pieces of 1.5mm cotton
string, about 12 inches (30 cm)
long

KNOTS & PATTERNS
Lark's Head Knot (page 16)

Alternating Square Knot
(page 28)

Double-Double Half Hitch
Diamond (page 36)

Square Knot with Multiple
Filler Cords (page 20)

Decreasing Alternating Square
Knot (page 29)

Tassels (page 38)

We have a special connection with this wall hanging because it is inspired by one of our first macramé creations. It has the perfect size to complement a decorative corner and create a nice composition with other ornaments.

Double diamonds play the main role in this piece. They are surrounded by a plain design which makes them shine. The way the tassels hang freely is an elegant detail to complete the geometric end of this piece.

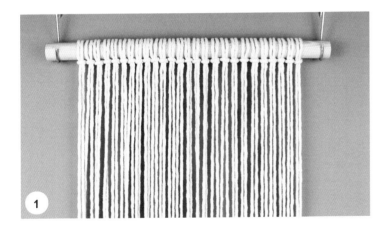

1. Attach all 24 pieces of the 98-inch (250-cm) cords onto the wooden dowel with the Lark's Head Knot.

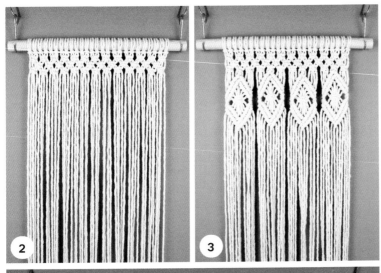

2. Begin the design by tying 3 rows of Alternating Square Knots.

3. In order to make 4 diamonds, take cords 6 and 7 (counting from left to right) to start tying Double-Double Half Hitch Diamonds. Once you do the 1st half of the diamond, tie a Square Knot with 6 filler cords inside it. Close the diamonds. Repeat the same with cords 18 and 19, 30 and 31, 42 and 43 to make 3 more Double-Double Half Hitch Diamonds.

4. Next, tie a row of Alternating Square Knots. Start tying so that the 1st row coincides with the bottom part of the diamonds. From the 2nd row on, start decreasing the design using the Decreasing Alternating Square Knot pattern. Do this until there are only 4 cords to tie the last Square Knot.

5. Make 7 tassels from the 12mm pieces of 12 inch (30 cm) cord. Use the 7 pieces of 1.5 mm cotton string (about 10 inches [25 cm] long) to tie them in the middle and the 7 pieces of 1.5mm cotton string (about 12 inches [30 cm] long) to make Gathering Knots. Attach them to the last row of Square Knots, leaving a space of 3.2 inches (8 cm) between the 1st 3 tassels and 2 inches (5 cm) for the one in the middle. Place the tassels and use a needle to help you pass the ends of the thin cord to the back part of the piece. Attach each tassel with a Double Half Hitch Knot.

6. Trim the ends slightly longer than the tassels in a V formation and brush them.

Mar Wall Hanging

Living near the sea is a blessing; the outstanding landscape that surrounds us is a constant source of inspiration that boosts our creativity and connection with nature. The Mar Wall Hanging combines the textures of the high seas and the calm waves reaching the shores serenely. The wooden beads bring a natural touch to complete and highlight the piece.

This is a perfect medium-sized wall hanging, full of details and layers. Sophisticated to the eye, you will definitely spend more time admiring it than the time it will take you to finish it!

FINISHED SIZE

30 inches long x 28 inches wide (75 cm long x 70 cm wide)

MATERIALS

Wooden dowel, 28 inches (70 cm) long

5mm single-twist cotton string, about 299 feet (91 m) total

1.5mm cotton string, about 122 inches (310 cm)

12mm single-twist cotton string, about 47 inches (120 cm)

36 wooden beads, 20mm diameter

CUTS

8 pieces of 5mm single-twist cotton string, 67 inches (170 cm) long

12 pieces of 5mm single-twist cotton string, 98 inches (250 cm) long

97 pieces of 5mm single-twist cotton string, 12 inches (30 cm), for the fringe

6 pieces of 5mm single-twist cotton string, 118 inches (300 cm) long

2 pieces of 1.5mm cotton string, 39.5 inches (100 cm) long, to hang the wooden beads

4 pieces of 12mm single-twist cotton string, 12 inches (30 cm) long, for the tassels

2 pieces of 1.5mm cotton strong, 10 inches (25 cm) long, for the tassels

2 pieces of 1.5mm cotton string, 12 inches (30 cm) long, for the tassels

KNOTS & PATTERNS

Lark's Head Knot (page 16)

Alternating Square Knot (page 28)

Diagonal Double Half Hitch Knot (page 22)

Diagonal Double Half Hitch Knot Diamond (page 36)

Square Knot with Multiple Filler Cords (page 20)

Square Knot Big Cluster (page 32)

Tassels (page 38)

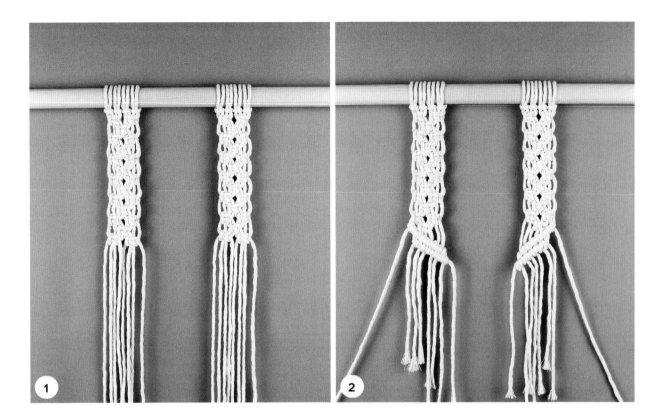

1. Attach the 8 pieces of the 67-inch (170-cm)-long cord onto the wooden dowel with the Lark's Head Knot. Place 4 cords on the left and 4 cords on the right at approximately 10 inches (25 cm) from the outer part of the dowel.

Use all the cords on the left to tie 12 rows of Alternating Square Knots. Repeat the same procedure with the cords on the right side of the dowel.

2. Take the outer cord from the design on the left as a guide. Tie Diagonal Double Half Hitches with all the cords. Then, leave the outer cord from the following row without knotting and tie another row of Diagonal Double Half Hitches. Repeat the same procedure on the right side of the design.

3. In order to join both parts of the design, take the 2 inner cords from each part, use the one on the right as a guide and the one on the left as the working cord to finish the design with a Double Half Hitch Knot. Trim the ends at the same length but don't worry too much about being perfect, because these cords will be hidden at the back of the design.

4. Attach 6 (98-inch [250-cm]-long) pieces of 5mm single-twist cotton onto the left side of the dowel with the Lark's Head Knot, leaving approximately 1 inch (2.5 cm) from the previous design. Take the 2 cords in the middle and use them to start tying a Diagonal Double Half Hitch Knot Diamond pattern with a Square Knot with Multiple Filler Cords inside the diamond pattern. Use 6 cords as filler cords and 2 cords to tie the Square Knot.

5. Take the 4 cords in the middle to tie a Square Knot Big Cluster.

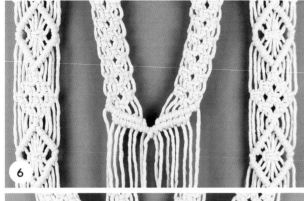

6. Make another Double Half Hitch Knot Diamond pattern with a Square Knot with Multiple Filler Cords inside it and another Square Knot Big Cluster.

Repeat steps 4 through 6 by attaching 6 more pieces of cord and repeating the patterns on the right side of the piece.

7. Join both parts of this second layer of the design by repeating steps 2 and 3.

8. Use the Lark's Head Knot to add fringe to the outer edges of each side, using the 5mm single-twist cotton strings that are 12-inch (30-cm) cords in each space. Attach 3 pieces at both top parts of the design and 6 pieces in the remaining spaces. Spaces are shown in the picture with arrows.

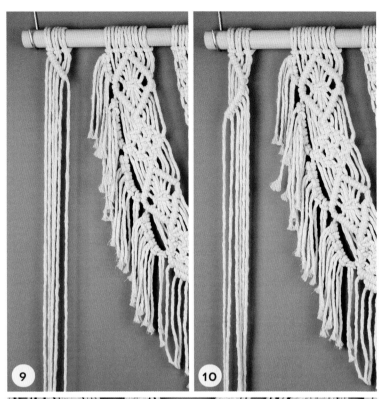

9. Attach 3 pieces of 5mm single-twist cotton string that are 118 inches (300 cm) long onto the left side of the wooden dowel with the Lark's Head Knot. Place them leaving approximately 1.2 inches (3 cm) from the previous design. Take the outer cord and use it as a guide to tie Diagonal Double Half Hitches to the right.

10. Continue using the same guiding cord and tie another row of Diagonal Double Half Hitches but this time place the guiding cord diagonally from the right to the left in order to form a zig-zag pattern.

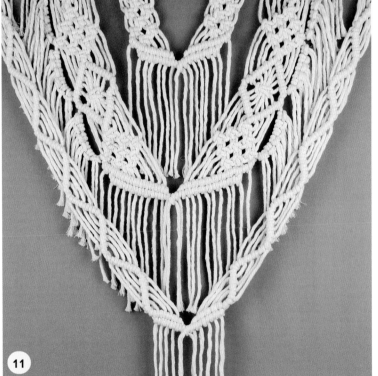

11. Keep on tying this pattern 13 more times. Make sure the last Diagonal Double Half Hitch row goes from the left to the right. Tie another row of Diagonal Double Half Hitches. Repeat steps 9 and 10 on the right side of the dowel, but this time start and finish the Diagonal Double Half Hitch rows from the right to the left. Join both pieces in the middle as in step 3 but this time, don't trim the ends because they will work as fringe.

12. Use the Lark's Head Knot to add fringe to the outer edges of each side. Tie 6 of the 12-inch (30-cm) cords in each space. Spaces are shown in the picture with arrows. Brush the ends.

13. Use the Lark's Head Knot to attach 1 piece of 1.5mm cotton string 39.5 inches (100 cm) long between the 1st and the 2nd layers of the design. Attach one on the left of the design and one on the right. Put tape on the ends of the cotton cords and pass 18 wooden beads through the cord on the left and 18 through the one on the right. Then join both sides in the middle with a Double Half Hitch Knot.

14. Make 2 tassels using 2 of the 12mm single-twist cotton string (12 inches [30 cm] long) pieces for each of them. Tie the pieces in the middle using the 1 piece of 1.5mm cotton string (10 inches [25 cm] long) for each tassel. To finish the tassels, tie them with a Gathering Knot using 1 piece of 1.5mm cotton string (12 inches [30 cm] long) for each of them. Use the cords on top of the tassels to attach them to the wall hanging. Place one of them where the wooden beads join and the other one where the last layer joins. Hang and delight your eyes!

Memories Wall Hanging

It's as if we share one mind, since our ideas usually come at the same time. Apart from being sisters, we have a very close connection, share thoughts, likes and dislikes . . . Have you ever experienced this with a friend or a relative? That is what happened to us when designing this piece, which was the first for the book.

If you are like us, braiding is something that we often did in childhood, and this project will take you to those nostalgic memories. The simplicity of these braids provides this macramé art piece with soft elegance and texture. You will definitely have fun while doing it and, as a medium-sized piece, it will look amazing in a cozy living room.

FINISHED SIZE

20 inches wide x 28 inches long (50 cm wide x 70 cm long)

MATERIALS

Wooden dowel, approximately 25.5 inches (65 cm) long

5mm single-twist cotton string, about 308 feet (94 m) total

CUTS

10 pieces, 126 inches (320 cm) long

8 pieces, 130 inches (330 cm) long

58 pieces, 24 inches (60 cm) long

1 piece, 28 inches (70 cm) long

KNOTS & PATTERNS

Lark's Head Knot (page 16)

Double Half Hitch Diamond Knot (page 35)

Square Knot (page 18)

Square Knot Sinnet (page 26)

Gathering Knot (page 23)

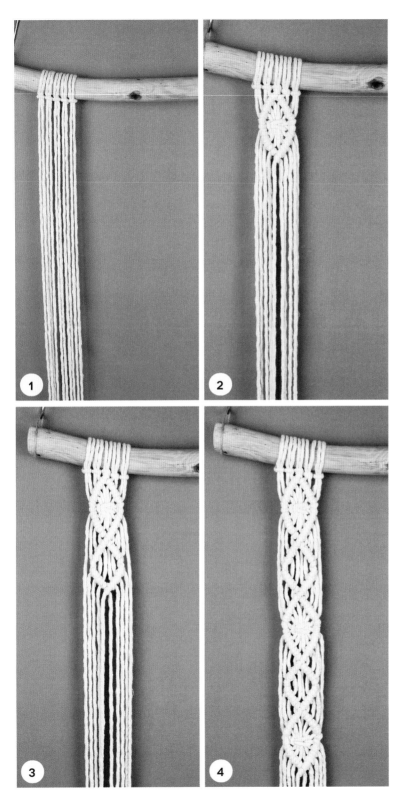

1. Tie 5 of the 126-inch (320-cm)-long cords onto the left end of the dowel using the Lark's Head Knot.

2. Start using the 2 cords in the middle and make a diamond pattern using Double Half Hitch Knots with a Square Knot inside the diamond.

3. Now, make a diamond pattern using only 8 cords. Leave 1 cord on the right and 1 on the left without knotting, as shown in the picture.

4. Repeat these patterns, alternating them until you get 3 diamonds with a Square Knot inside and two smaller diamonds.

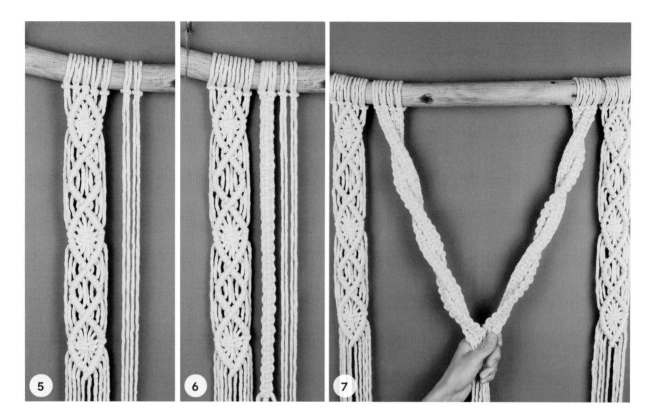

5. Tie 2 pieces of 130-inch (330-cm)-long cord using the Lark's Head Knot on the right side of the pattern you have already done, leaving 1.2 inches (3 cm) in between. When forming the Lark's Head Knot, fold the cords so that the 2 inner cords are 47 inches (120 cm) long; remember these are just filler cords, so the outer cords should be longer since they are the working cords.

6. Make a Square Knot Sinnet of 30 knots, approximately 17 inches (42 cm) in length. Repeat step 5, attaching 2 more cords (130 inches [330 cm] long) with the Lark's Head Knot next to the previous Square Knot Sinnet to make a new Square Knot Sinnet.

Repeat everything you have done in this step up to this point, but now on the right side of the dowel.

At this point, we suggest you place the wall hanging on a flat surface so it is easier for you to continue with the following steps.

7. Braid the 2 Square Knot Sinnets on the left, crossing them up to the end and do the same with the 2 Square Knots Sinnets on the right.

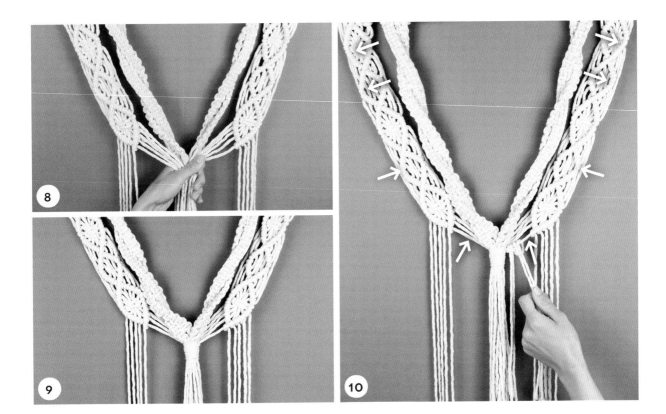

8. Join everything in the middle. Take only the 5 inner cords from each of the diamond patterns, leaving the outer 5 as part of the fringe.

9. Use 1 piece of 28-inch (70-cm)-long cord to tie everything with a Gathering Knot.

10. Use the Lark's Head Knot to add fringe to the outer edges of each side. Tie the 24-inch (60-cm) cords in each space. Spaces are shown in the picture with arrows.

Your wall hanging is done! If you like, you can brush the ends.

waterfall wall hanging

This geometric design has a delicate beauty in its simplicity and the tassels add a perfect complement that balances the texture of the piece. We immediately fell in love with how the tassels naturally fell, resembling a majestic waterfall. It's pure inspiration! Brushing the tassels may work as a kind of therapy. Think about a subtle waterfall while making them and your mind will take an insightful journey that will definitely relax you!

FINISHED SIZE
24 inches long x 13 inches wide (60 cm long x 32 cm wide)

MATERIALS
Wooden dowel, 18 inches (45 cm) long

5mm single-twist cotton string, about 230 feet (70 m) total

12mm single-twist cotton string, about 99 inches (250 cm) total

CUTS
25 pieces of 5mm single-twist cotton string, 110 inches (280 cm) long

10 pieces of 12mm single-twist cotton string, 10 inches (25 cm) long, for the tassels

KNOTS & PATTERNS
Lark's Head Knot (page 16)

Double Half Hitch Knot Diamond (page 35)

Square Knot (page 18)

Diagonal Double Half Hitch (page 22)

1. Attach the 25 pieces of 110-inch (280-cm)-long cord onto the wooden dowel with the Lark's Head Knot.

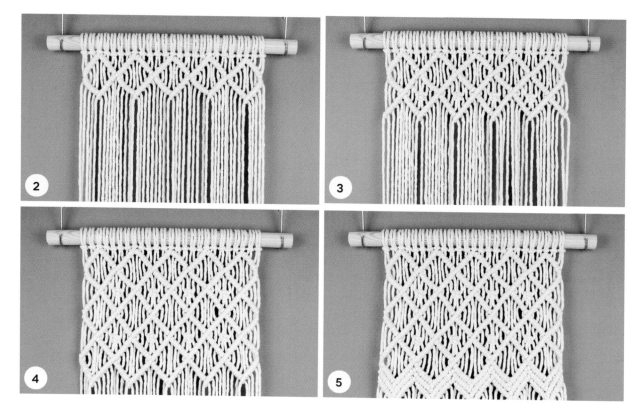

2. In order to start the design, leave the first 4 cords on the left without tying. Take the 2 following cords and tie a Double Half Hitch Knot Diamond. After that, take 2 cords every 8 cords to tie 4 more Double Half Hitch Knot Diamonds.

3. In the 2nd row of diamonds, tie 1 Square Knot inside them. Continue using the same guiding cords from the previous diamonds to tie another row of Double Half Hitch Knot Diamonds.

4. Continue tying diamonds alternating between these 2 patterns until you get 3 rows of Double Half Hitch Knot Diamonds and 2 rows of Double Half Hitch Knot Diamonds with a Square Knot inside them.

5. Once you reach the last row of diamonds, tie 2 more rows of Diagonal Double Half Hitches close to them.

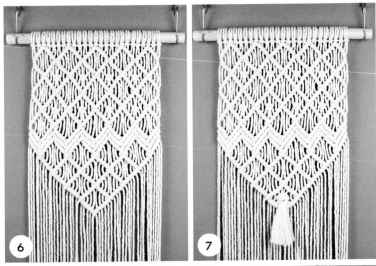

6. Now we will make Double Half Hitch Knot Diamonds to place the tassels inside them. First make a row of 4 diamonds, and then tie 3 diamonds. Then make a row of 2 diamonds and, finally, tie 1 diamond.

7. Add tassels to the piece using the 12mm pieces of cotton cord. Start from the one at the bottom. Trim and comb each tassel before placing the following one.

8. Trim the ends of the pieces at 24 inches (60 cm) from the dowel and brush the ends.

PeaRL WaLL Hanging

Wherever you go in Mallorca, our home city in Spain, you will certainly come across pearls. They are a distinctive element of the island and a source of inspiration for us. We found wooden beads offer the perfect way to include the elegance of pearls in our projects.

The combination of tassels with wooden beads and the natural look of the driftwood make this piece stylish and suitable for any bohemian home. You will make a lovely piece in a few simple steps with a stunning result!

1. Attach the 8 pieces of 5mm single-twist cotton string 79 inches (200 cm) long onto the wooden dowel with the Lark's Head Knot at the center of the dowel.

FINISHED SIZE
25 inches long x 24 inches wide (65 cm long x 60 cm wide)

MATERIALS
Wooden dowel or driftwood, 24 inches (60 cm) long

5mm single-twist cotton string, about 230 feet (70 m) total

12mm single-twist cotton string, about 108 inches (275 cm) total

1.5mm cotton string, about 63 inches (160 cm) total

32 wooden beads, 20mm diameter

High-quality Scotch or masking tape

CUTS
8 pieces of 5mm single-twist cotton string, 79 inches (200 cm) long

10 pieces of 5mm single-twist cotton string, 118 inches (300 cm) long

46 pieces of 5mm single-twist cotton string, 20 inches (50 cm) long, for the fringe

11 pieces of 12mm single-twist cotton string, 10 inches (25 cm) long, for the tassels

2 pieces of 1.5mm 31.5 inches (80 cm) long, to hang the wooden beads

KNOTS & PATTERNS
Lark's Head Knot (page 16)

Double-Double Half Hitch Diamond (page 36)

Square Knot Big Cluster (page 32)

Double Half Hitch Diamond (page 35)

Double Half Hitch Knot (page 21)

Tassels (page 38)

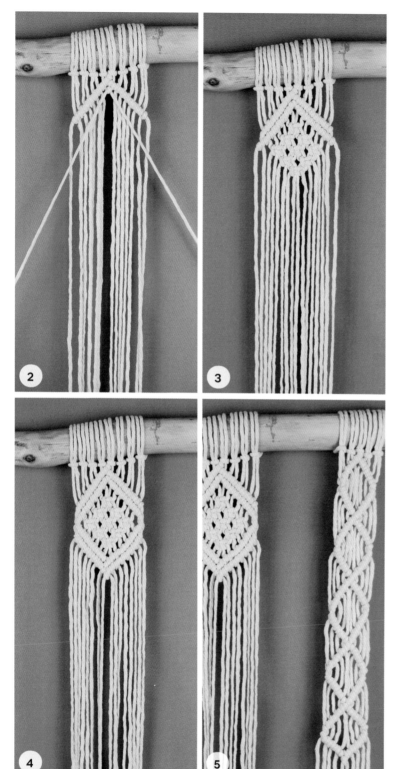

2. Take the 2 cords in the middle and start tying a Double-Double Half Hitch Diamond.

3. Use the 4 cords in the middle of the diamond and tie a Square Knot Big Cluster. Start it at approximately 0.4 inch (1 cm) from the Double Half Hitches row so that the cluster is in the middle of the diamond and you can make the design accurately.

4. Finish the Double-Double Half Hitch Diamond, using the same outer cords you used for the previous rows as a guide.

5. Attach 10 pieces of 5mm single-twist cotton string 118 inches (300 cm) long onto the wooden dowel with the Lark's Head Knot. Place 5 of them on the left side of the dowel and the remaining 5 cords on the right side of the dowel. Attach them at approximately 3.2 inches (8 cm) from the outer part. Take the 2 cords in the middle and make a sequence of 5 Double Half Hitch Diamonds.

6. In order to join both parts, take the 2 inner cords from each piece and tie them with a Double Half Hitch Knot. Use this knot as the starting point of a Double Half Hitch Diamond. Tie it close to the diamonds on both sides.

7. Use the Lark's Head Knot to add fringe to the outer edges of each side, using the 20-inch (50-cm) cords in each space. Attach 3 pieces at the top part of the design and 5 pieces in the remaining spaces. Brush the ends.

8. Use the 11 pieces of 12mm single-twist cotton string (10 inches [25 cm] long) and add a tassel inside each diamond.

9. Use the Lark's Head Knot to attach 2 pieces of 1.5mm cotton string 31.5 inches (80 cm) long between the 1st and the 2nd layers of the design closer to the outer design. Attach one on the left of the piece and one on the right. Put tape in the ends of the cotton cords and thread 16 wooden beads on both pieces. Then join both sides in the middle with a Double Half Hitch Knot.

SUNFLOWER MIRROR

FINISHED SIZE
18 inches (45 cm) diameter

MATERIALS
5mm single-twist cotton string, about 158 feet (48 m) total

Metal ring, 7.5 inches (19 cm) diameter

Round mirror, 8 inches (20 cm) diameter

1.5mm cotton string, about 6 inches (15 cm) total

Strong contact adhesive glue

CUTS
48 pieces of 5mm single-twist cotton string, 39.5 inches (100 cm) long

1 piece of 1.5mm cotton string, 6 inches (15 cm)

KNOTS & PATTERNS
Lark's Head Knot (page 16)

Square Knot (page 18)

Decreasing Square Knot (page 29)

Double Half Hitch Knot (page 21)

Diagonal Double Half Hitch Knot (page 22)

Mirrors are a must in every single house, and we generally have more than one at home in different rooms. So, if you want to give a twist to your mirrors, this project is for you! This one is a nice piece to tackle when you are new to macramé, and you will definitely surprise your family and friends with this enchanted project. Who knows, maybe you will end up making a wonderful combination of mirrors on an empty wall. They look really good in pairs.

We named this project Sunflower Mirror since its shape and fringe resemble that pure and gorgeous plant—don't you think so?

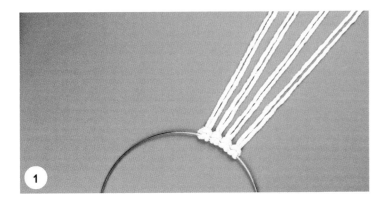

1. Working on a flat surface, use the Lark's Head Knot to attach all of the 5mm single-twist cotton cords onto the metal ring.

2. Make a 1st row of Square Knots.

3. Divide the design into 6 groups of 4 Square Knots. Make a Decreasing Square Knot pattern in each set.

4. Use the outer cords from each set to join them with a simple Half Hitch Knot.

5. Continue using those cords as guiding cords to tie Diagonal Double Half Hitches around the Decreasing Square Knot pattern done in step 3. Join both guiding cords in the middle with a Double Half Hitch Knot to close the design.

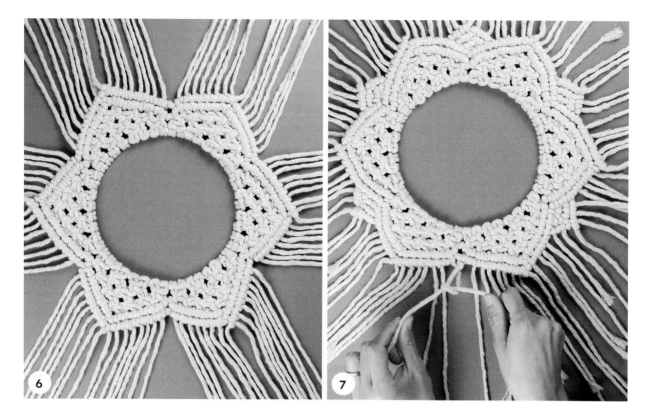

6. In order to make another row of Diagonal Double Half Hitches, repeat steps 4 and 5.

7. Take the 2 outer cords from each design and tie a Double Half Hitch Knot. Then, tie 2 more rows of Diagonal Double Half Hitches using the following 2 outer cords.

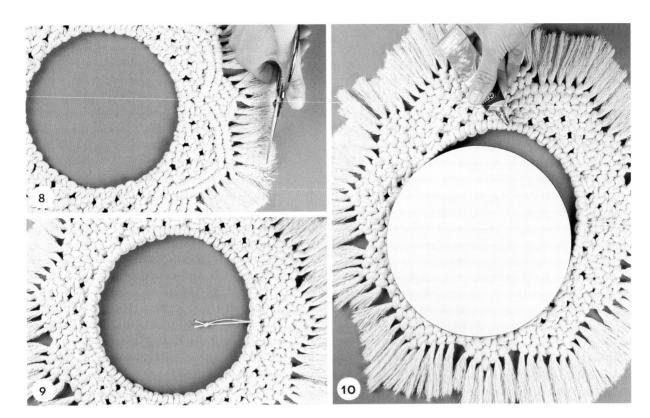

8. Trim the ends to about 1¼ inch (3 cm) and brush the ends.

9. In order to be able to hang the mirror on the wall, attach the 6-inch (15-cm) piece of cord to the ring using the Lark's Head Knot and tie the ends tightly. In order to keep the string hidden behind the macramé when hanging it, make sure the loop isn't longer than the knotted surface.

10. Use the contact adhesive to stick the mirror to the macramé piece. Follow the manufacturer's instructions of the adhesive you are working with in order to use it accurately.

APRIL SHELF

We live in Europe and April is one of our favorite months since flowers delight our eyes everywhere we go. Spring is by far THE season of love, inspiration and hope. We named this project April Shelf since the combination of clusters looks like flowers on a painting, and "flowers" is a synonym for spring.

When it comes to shelves, we always tend to use the same kind of holders, that's why this project is a perfectly fashionable alternative. You can highlight its unique design with some modern and stylish ornaments or with just a couple of plants. This project is suitable for many rooms in the house—where will you place it?

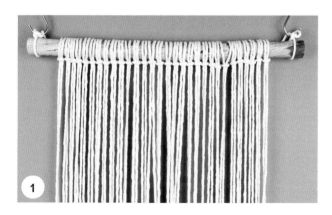

1. Attach all 30 pieces of the 98-inch (250-cm)-long cord onto the wooden dowel with the Lark's Head Knot.

FINISHED SIZE

24 inches long x 16 inches wide
(60 cm long x 40 cm wide)

MATERIALS

Wooden dowel, 20 inches
(50 cm) long

5mm single-twist cotton string, about 285 feet (87 m) total

Piece of wood, 20 inches long x 4 inches wide (50 cm long x 10 cm wide)

CUTS

30 pieces of 5mm single-twist cotton string, 98 inches (250 cm) long

4 pieces of 5mm single-twist cotton string, 118 inches (300 cm) long

KNOTS & PATTERNS

Lark's Head Knot (page 16)

Square Knot Diamond (page 34)

Square Knot Small Cluster (page 33)

Square Knot Big Cluster (page 32)

Square Knot Sinnet (page 26)

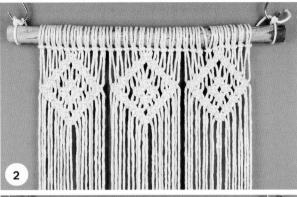

2. Make a Square Knot Diamond every 10 cords with a Square Knot Small Cluster inside it. You'll get 3 Square Knot Diamonds.

3. Start from the left side of the design and take cords 19, 20, 21 and 22. Leave a space of 1 inch (2.5 cm) from the diamonds to tie a Square Knot Big Cluster between the first 2 diamonds. Repeat the same procedure with cords 39, 40, 41 and 42. Finally, leave 1 inch (2.5 cm) from the diamond in the middle and make another Square Knot Big Cluster below it.

4. Tie Square Knot Small Clusters below the 2 outer diamonds leaving a space of 1 inch (2.5 cm) from them. Tie 1 Square Knot at 2.8 inches (7 cm) from each big cluster above.

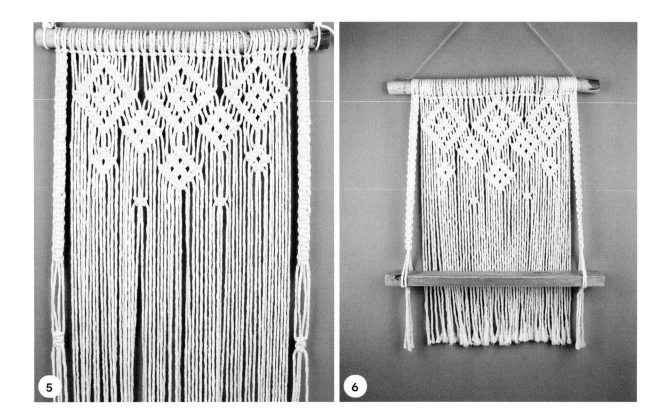

5. Attach 2 of the 118-inch (300-cm)-long pieces onto the left outer part of the dowel with the Lark's Head Knot. Fold the cords so that the inner cords are 39.5 inches (100 cm) long and the outer cords are 79 inches (200 cm) long. Remember inner cords are only filler cords and the outer cords will be the working cords. Tie a Square Knot Sinnet that is 14 inches (35 cm) long. Then, leave a space of 5 inches (12 cm) without tying (this is where the wood piece will go) and finally tie 2 Square Knots. Repeat the same procedure on the right outer side of the design.

6. Trim the ends at the same length and finally place the wood piece by passing it through the space without knots in the Square Knot sinnet.

FROM THE CEILING

Plant hangers are the macramé décor pieces that we think represent the revival of this fiber art best. They played a very important role during the '70s when macramé was so popular, but after that, their popularity faded away for a while. Nowadays, they have come back to the scene with a refreshed and modern look!

We love the way in which macramé plant hangers highlight the presence of plants inside a room and can even help you to create a green corner at home. Here, you'll find three completely different plant hangers (page 103, page 107 and page 111) with a stylish design that will make you love plants even if you don't have a green thumb. We also decided to include a lamp (page 115) and a swing (page 119) in this section for you to see that some designs may seem very intricate and complex, but they aren't!

Finding eye-catching pieces to hang from the ceiling and make your spaces look modern is no longer a hard task . . . these projects show that macramé art makes for the best boho accents. You'll soon be decorating your whole home with these handmade beauties!

Magnolia Plant Hanger

Plants by their very nature are so stunning, and this plant hanger perfectly complements their elegant beauty with a boho touch given by the wooden beads. We personally like how this pothos and the hanger complement each other in a charming way.

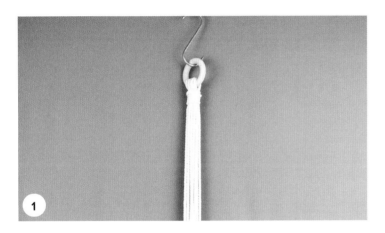

1. Fold the 8 pieces of 79-inch (200-cm)-long cord in the middle and pass them through the wooden ring. Fasten them with a Gathering Knot close to the ring using 1 of the 16-inch (40-cm)-long cords.

FINISHED SIZE
35.5 inches (90 cm) long

MATERIALS
3mm 3-strand twisted cotton cord, about 103 feet (31.2 m) total

Wooden ring, 3 inches (7 cm) diameter

24 wooden beads, 20 mm diameter

1.5mm cotton string, about 13.2 feet (4 m) total

CUTS
8 pieces of 3mm twisted cotton cord, 79 inches (200 cm) long

2 pieces of 3mm twisted cotton cord, 16 inches (40 cm) long

48 pieces of 3mm twisted cotton cord, 12 inches (30 cm) long

4 pieces of 1.5mm cotton string, 39.5 inches (100 cm) long

KNOTS & PATTERNS
Gathering Knot (page 23)

Square Knot (page 18)

Lark's Head Knot (page 16)

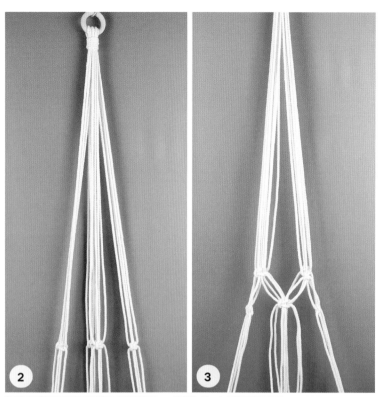

2. Take 4 cords and tie a Square Knot 24 inches (60 cm) from the ring. Repeat the same with the rest of the cords.

3. Now, take 2 cords from one of the Square Knots you have just tied and 2 cords from the Square Knot immediately next to it. Use those 4 cords to tie another Square Knot, leaving 2.5 inches (6 cm) from the previous ones. In this step, we are joining the design.

4. In order to close the hanger, take all the cords together, except the 2 cords which are in the middle of each Square Knot. Tie a Gathering Knot at 3.2 inches (8 cm) from the last Square Knots, using the other 16-inch (40-cm)-long cord.

5. For this step, we advise you to place a pot inside the hanger to make it easier to attach the following cords. Take the 48 cords of 3 mm twisted cotton cord (12 inches [30 cm] long) and attach them to the hanger with the Lark's Head Knot. You should place 12 cords on each of the 4 sides of the hanger, in the spaces between the Square Knots.

6. Finish the design with the wooden beads. Attach the 4 pieces of 1.5mm cotton string (39.5 inches [100 cm] long) from the 1st Square Knots using a Half Hitch Knot. Thread 6 beads on each string (24 beads total), and attach the ends with a Half Hitch Knot.

Succulent Plant Hanger

This plant hanger is a variation to the typical style because it is a combination of a wall hanging with a plant hanger. Succulents are perfect for this kind of hanger—they look great in pairs due to their wide variety of shapes and colors.

This piece starts as a wall hanging since you need a dowel and a simple design, and it finishes with two spaces to hold pots. It's such a fun project—we are sure you will enjoy making it!

FINISHED SIZE

13 inches wide x 30 inches long (32 cm wide x 75 cm long)

MATERIALS

Wooden dowel, 18 inches (45 cm) long

5mm single-twist cotton string, about 217 feet (66 m) total

Plant pot, 3.5 inches (9 cm) diameter (suggested size)

CUTS

26 pieces of 5mm single-twist cotton string, 98 inches (250 cm) long

2 pieces of 5mm single-twist cotton string, 18 inches (45 cm) long

KNOTS & PATTERNS

Lark's Head Knot (page 16)

Alternating Square Knot (page 28)

Decreasing Square Knot (page 29)

Diagonal Double Half Hitch Knot (page 22)

Double Half Hitch Knot (page 21)

Square Knot Big Cluster (page 32)

Square Knot Small Cluster (page 33)

Gathering Knot (page 23)

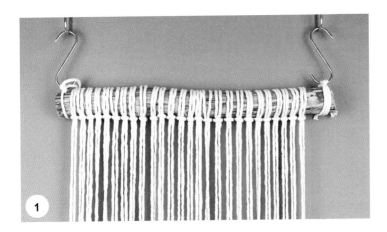

1. Attach all 26 pieces of the 98-inch (250-cm)-long cord onto the wooden dowel with the Lark's Head Knot.

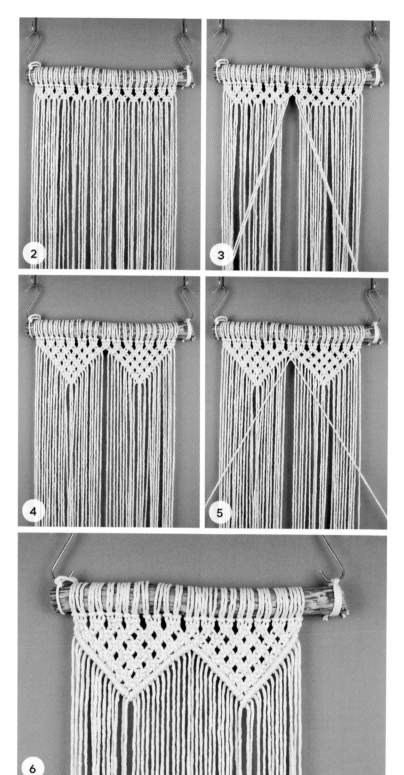

2. Begin the design by tying 2 rows of Alternating Square Knots.

3. In order to divide the design in two to make 2 V-shapes of Square Knots, take the 4 cords in the middle (cords 25, 26, 27 and 28) and leave them without knotting.

4. Start decreasing the Square Knots design on both sides by leaving 2 cords every time you begin and finish a new row, until there are only 4 cords to tie a Square Knot.

5. Use the 2 cords in the middle of the piece and make a Double Half Hitch Knot in order to join both V-shapes.

6. Tie 1 row of Diagonal Double Half Hitches close to the previous pattern using the outer and inner cords of the design as guiding cords.

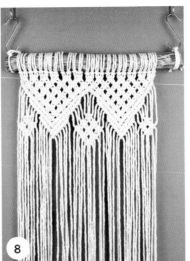

7. For the next Diagonal Double Half Hitch row, leave 4 cords at the beginning without tying in order to make a shorter row. Finally, leave the other 4 cords without tying and make another Diagonal Double Half Hitch row. Repeat this process for both V-shapes.

8. Take the 4 cords in the middle of the piece (cords 25, 26, 27 and 28) and start making a Square Knot Big Cluster at 2 inches (5 cm) from the joint of the V-shapes. Also make 2 Square Knot Small Clusters in the outer parts of the design using the 8 outer cords. Start them at the same height as the Big Cluster.

9. Use 2 cords from the Big Cluster and 2 outer cords and tie a Square Knot at 9 inches (22 cm) from the design above. Tie a Big Cluster using the cords at the back. In this way, we create the pot holder form. Do this on both sides of the work so you have 2 pot holder forms.

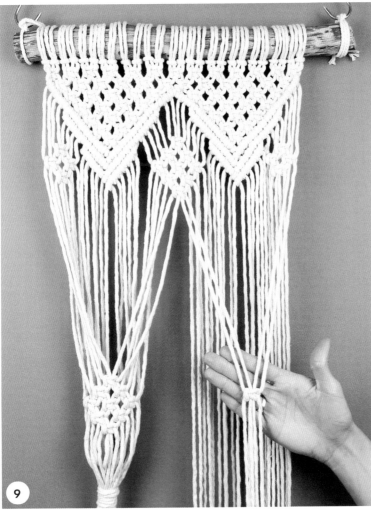

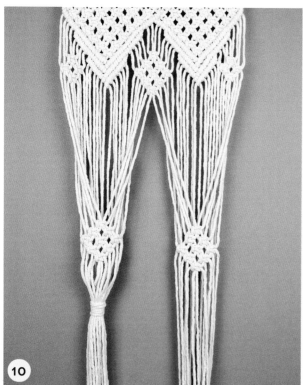

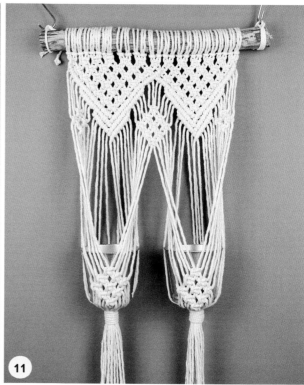

10. Use the 2 pieces of 5mm single-twist cotton string 18 inches (45 cm) long to finish the design by closing it with Gathering Knots on both sides.

11. Place your plant pots inside the plant hanger to finish!

CHANDELIER HANGER

Let's go a step beyond plant hangers' traditional designs with this fantastic and unique hanger. We particularly like the way in which the design embraces the element inside it, and the cords falling from both sides add a special movement that completes the uniqueness of this hanger. It is ideal for either a plant or a jar, but it also looks stunning with a candle.

Its design is absolutely different from the other hangers since we generally start them with a ring and knot downwards. In this case, you will begin with a plain design and the wooden ring will be included at the end. Does it sound weird? Well, we assure you will have a great time trying it!

FINISHED SIZE
43 inches (110 cm) long

MATERIALS
5mm single-twist cotton string, about 177 feet (54 m)

High-quality Scotch or masking tape

Wooden ring, 3 inches (7 cm) diameter

CUTS
2 pieces of 5mm single-twist cotton string, 79 inches (200 cm) long

28 pieces of 5mm single-twist cotton string, 67 inches (170 cm) long

2 pieces of 5mm single-twist cotton string, 39.5 inches (100 cm) long

KNOTS & PATTERNS
Double Half Hitch Knot (page 22)

Alternating Square Knot (page 28)

Half Knot Sinnet (page 24)

Gathering Knot (page 23)

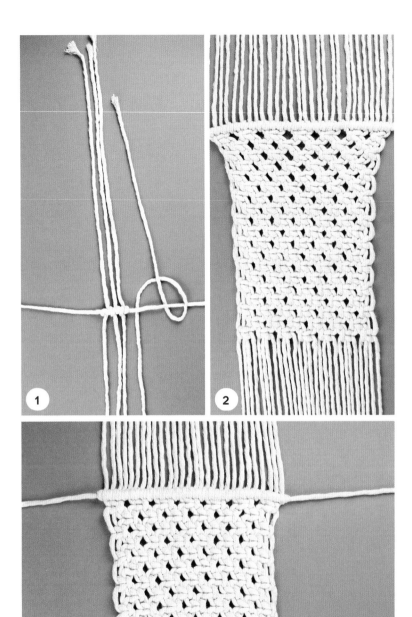

1. Use 1 of the 79-inch (200-cm)-long pieces as the guiding cord and place it on a flat work surface. Attach it to the work surface with tape or something similar so it doesn't move. Attach the 28 pieces of 67-inch (170 cm)-long cord in the middle of the guiding cord with Double Half Hitches, leaving an end of 20 inches (50 cm) that will work as the fringe of the piece.

2. Use the longer cords to tie 19 rows of Alternating Square Knots.

3. Place the other 79-inch (200-cm)-long cord immediately after the Alternating Square Knots, making it sure that it is in the middle. Tie Double Half Hitches around the guiding cord.

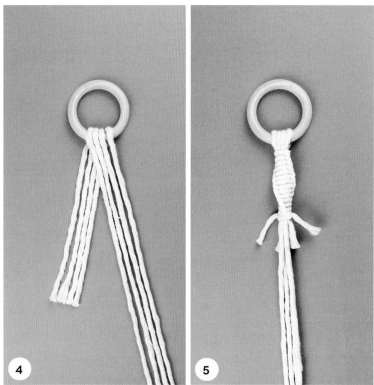

4. Gather the ends of the guiding cords and pass them through the wooden ring.

5. Use 1 of the pieces of 39.5-inch (100-cm)-long cord as a working cord. Fold it in half so that you get the same length for each side and tie a Half Knot Sinnet of 14 knots around the gathered cords—these work as filler cords.

6. Take the other piece of 39.5-inch (100-cm)-long cord and fasten the design with a Gathering Knot. Your hanger is finished!

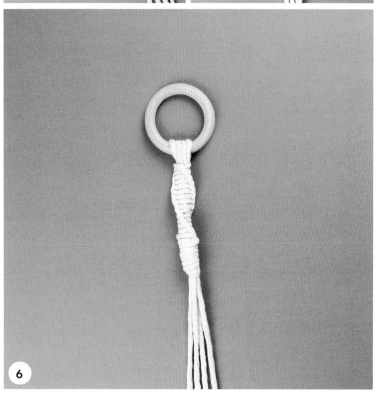

sunset Lamp

Delightful to the eyes, sunsets are unique in their nature—the light that reaches us fills us with comfort and peace and makes us feel at home. That feeling is similar to the one we have when we are calm and enjoying the subtle light this lamp emanates. This piece is elegant in its simplicity and it's perfect to add a warm, cozy and peaceful accent to any room.

FINISHED SIZE

14 inches diameter x 20 inches long (35 cm diameter x 50 cm long)

MATERIALS

Round hanging lamp frame, 14 inches (35 cm)

5mm single-twist cotton string, about 565 feet (172 m total)

CUTS

86 pieces, 79 inches (200 cm) long

KNOTS & PATTERNS

Lark's Head Knot (page 16)

Alternating Square Knot (page 28)

Square Knot Alternating Inner and Outer Cords (page 31)

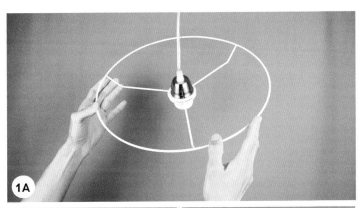

1. Hang the lamp structure and attach all the cords onto the circular structure with the Lark's Head Knot.

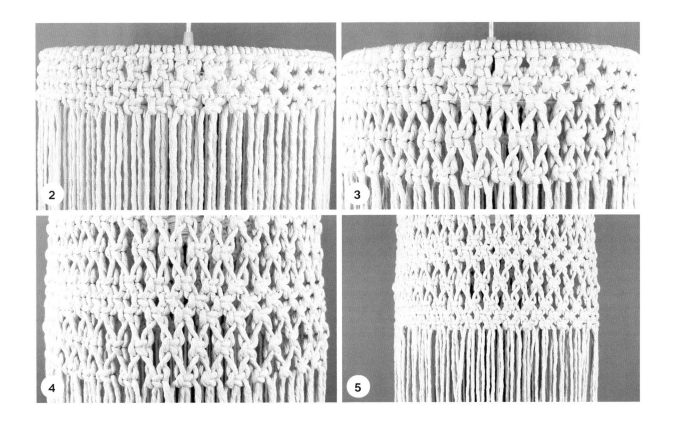

2. Tie 3 rows of Alternating Square Knots. Try to tie the knots close to each other, but don't fasten them too tight in order to prevent the design from narrowing.

3. Leave a space of 1 inch (2.5 cm) and tie 2 rows of Square Knots, alternating the inner and outer cords.

4. Tie 2 more rows of Alternating Square Knots and then repeat step 3 to make another 2 rows of Square Knots, alternating the inner and outer cords.

5. Complete the design by doing step 2 again. Trim the ends at the same length and brush them.

SOFia SWiN9

Even though they are simple objects, swings have an amazing power . . . In the very moment that you sit on one and start balancing, you begin to feel a subtle breeze in your body and your hair moves freely, making you experience a peace and freedom like when you swayed on a swing as a child. Probably lots of good memories come to your mind! We named this piece after our niece, Sofia, because she reminds us of when we were little girls enjoying those simple, free-spirited moments.

In this project, you'll put several of your macramé skills into practice, and the result will be a beautiful and delicate swing with different textures. This swing will be perfectly suitable for photography settings, kids' parties, weddings or even simply to enjoy at home!

KNOTS & PATTERNS

Lark's Head Knot (page 16)

Alternating Square Knot (page 28)

Square Knot Diamond (page 34)

Square Knot Small Cluster (page 33)

Square Knot Big Cluster (page 32)

Gathering Knot (page 23)

Double Half Hitch Knot (page 21)

FINISHED SIZE

20 inches long x 16 inches wide (50 cm long x 40 cm wide)

MATERIALS

Wooden dowel, at least 24 inches (60 cm) long (only needed to knot the design, then taken off)

5mm single-twist cotton string, about 260 feet (79 m) total

10mm jute rope, about 26 feet (8 m) total

Piece of wood, 17.7 x 8 inches (45 x 20 cm)

2 metal rings, 2 inches (5 cm) diameter

Electric drill and 10mm drill bit

CUTS

32 pieces of 5mm single-twist cotton string, 87 inches (220 cm) long

16 pieces of 5mm single-twist cotton string, 14 inches (35 cm) long

2 pieces of 5mm single-twist cotton string, 39.5 inches (100 cm) long

2 pieces of 10mm jute rope, 157.5 inches (400 cm) long

2 pieces of 5mm single-twist cotton string, 20 inches (50 cm) long

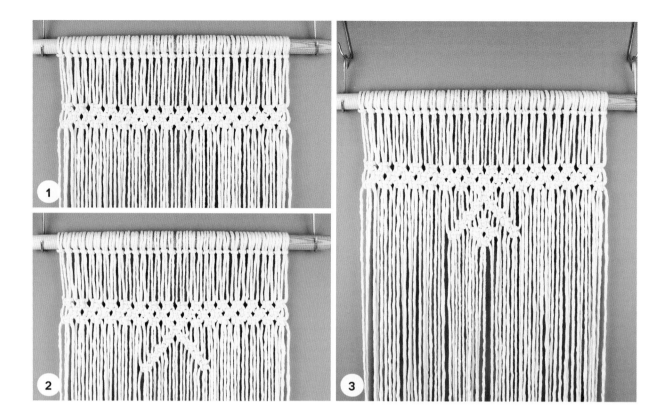

1. Attach the 32 pieces of 87-inch (220-cm)-long cord onto the wooden dowel with the Lark's Head Knot. You will only need to use the dowel to hang the design while knotting; once it is finished, you'll take the macramé off of the dowel. Leave a space of 4 inches (10 cm) from the dowel and start the design by tying 3 rows of Alternating Square Knots.

2. Take cords 31, 32, 33 and 34 and tie a Square Knot. Use it as the beginning of a Square Knot Diamond of 4 Square Knots. Tie only half the diamond.

3. Once you have half the diamond, take the 4 cords in the middle of it and tie a Square Knot Small Cluster inside the diamond.

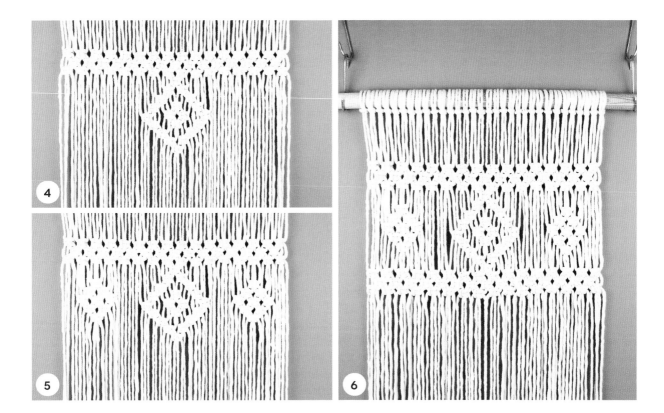

4. Finish the Square Knot Diamond.

5. Start from the left side of the pattern taking cords 9, 10, 11 and 12 and tie a Square Knot Big Cluster at approximately 1.2 inches (3 cm) from the pattern above.

In order to repeat the same pattern on the right side of the piece, take cords 53, 54, 55 and 56 and tie a Square Knot Big Cluster.

6. To make a symmetric and consistent pattern, repeat step 2. Try to keep the same space from the big clusters, and make sure the 1st row of Square Knots coincides with the bottom of the Square Knot Diamond.

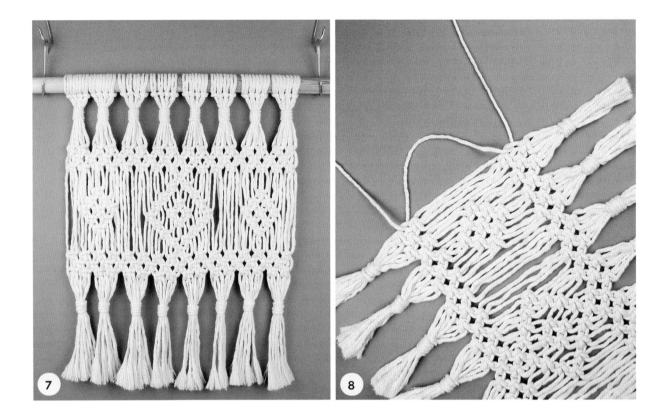

7. Leave a space of 2 inches (5 cm) from the design and tie a Gathering Knot every 8 cords using the 14-inch (35-cm)-long pieces. Do the same on both sides of the design.

8. Take the piece off the dowel. Trim the ends at the same length and brush them. Pass the pieces of 39.5-inch (100-cm)-long cotton cord through the space at the beginning of the 2nd Square Knots row. Use one cord for each side. With these cords you will attach the macramé piece to the wood.

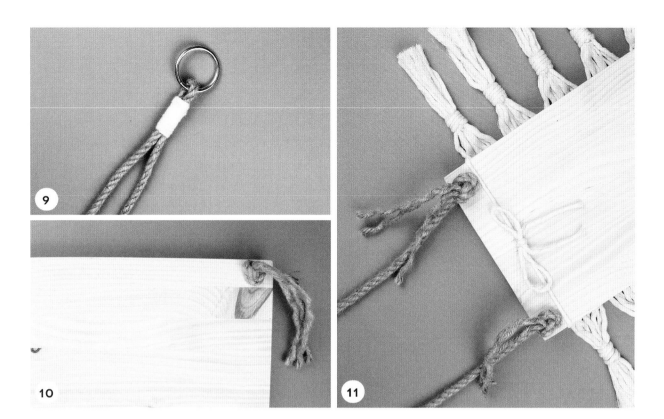

PREPARE THE SWING

We used pine tree wood for this project, but any type of wood will work as well. We advise you to sand the wood before you start assembling the swing in order to avoid possible injuries and to make it safe for kids too.

9. Pass 1 of the jute ropes through 1 of the metal rings and fold the rope in the middle holding the ring. Use a piece of 5mm cotton cord 20 inches (50 cm) long to fasten the ropes and the ring with a Gathering Knot. Repeat the same with the other ring and rope.

10. Using the electric drill and 10mm drill bit, drill 1 hole in every corner of the wood at 0.6 inch (1.5 cm) from the outer part. Thread the ends of the jute rope through the holes in the wooden piece and make regular knots below the wood. Make sure all the knots are done at the same length.

11. Place the macramé piece on the swing and attach it to the wood using the cords added in step 8. Make a Double Half Hitch Knot and then a simple bow to hold them together.

IN the BEDROOM

The bedroom is a place that makes us feel secure, calm and free from the outer world. It's a place where you relax and that we particularly love decorating. The selection of accents for this space should not be overwhelming to the eyes. They should subtly invite you to rest. That's why we have created a collection of macramé pieces suitable for a bedroom in which every detail is taken into account to warmly embrace its guests.

A stunning headboard (page 127), with its natural texture and beauty, will become the main character in the bedroom and will make it look cozy and sophisticated at the same time! A rug (page 135) and a curtain (page 131) will make your room look fresh and elegant. Combined with other textures, they will definitely highlight your space in a stylish manner. But don't hesitate to place them in any other space of your home! We adore the delightful movement of curtains in a gallery, and rugs are perfect for a home entrance too. Let your hands make magic and have a great time creating these unique pieces!

IMPERIAL Headboard

Some pieces have that stunning look that immediately makes you think about majestic and admirable things. When working with large macramé designs, you find yourself creating pieces of art which have that imposing elegance. This headboard is the case of a perfect accent for your bedroom with that delicate and simple but magnificent touch that will highlight your queen-size bed!

1. As you'll be working with very long cords, we suggest that you tape the ends so that they don't unravel as you go. Attach all 100 pieces of the 146-inch (370-cm)-long cord onto the dowel with the Lark's Head Knot.

FINISHED SIZE

5 feet wide x 31.5 inches long (1.40 m wide x 80 cm) long

MATERIALS

Wooden dowel, 5.5 feet (1.6 m) long

3mm 3-strand twisted cotton cord, about 1,214 feet (370 m) total

High-quality Scotch or masking tape

CUTS

100 pieces, 146 inches (370 cm) long

KNOTS & PATTERNS

Lark's Head Knot (page 16)

Half Knot Sinnet (page 24)

Alternating Square Knot (page 28)

Square Knot Diamond (page 34)

Square Knot Small Cluster (page 33)

Square Knot Big Cluster (page 32)

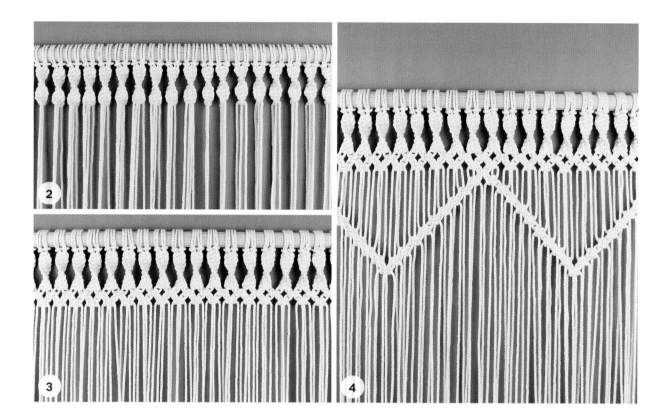

2. Start the design by taking the first 4 cords to make a Half Knot Sinnet of 10 Half Knots. Then, repeat the same with the remaining cords until you have a total of 50 Half Knot Sinnets.

3. Leaving the first 2 cords without tying, tie 2 rows of Alternating Square Knots. Tie them tight and close to the sinnets.

4. Starting from the left of the design, use cord numbers 19, 20, 21 and 22 to tie the 1st Square Knot of a Square Knot Diamond. Then, tie 9 Square Knots on each side of the diamond. As this diamond has a pattern inside, you only have to make a half diamond up to now. Repeat the same with cords 59, 60, 61, 62; again with cords 99, 100, 101, 102; again with cords 139, 140, 141, 142; and lastly with cords 179, 180, 181, 182. You should now have a total of 5 half diamonds. Since these diamonds are one next to the other, a 10th Square Knot will be the one that joins them.

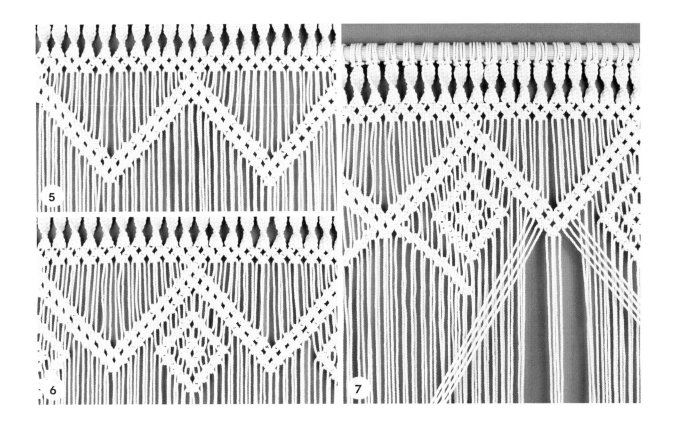

5. Make another row of Square Knots close to the previous one.

6. Now, we are going to make a smaller Square Knot Diamond with a Square Knot Small Cluster inside it. Take the 4 cords in the middle of the bigger half diamond and leave 2 inches (5 cm) from it to start a smaller Square Knot Diamond of 5 knots. Once you have done half the diamond, take the 4 cords in the middle of it and leave 1.2 inches (3 cm) to tie a Square Knot Small Cluster. Then finish the small diamond. Repeat the same in the other diamonds.

7. Now, it is time to close the big diamonds! Starting from the left of the design, leave the first 2 cords without tying and tie the 1st row of the diamond. For the following diamonds, leave the 4 cords in the middle where the diamonds join without tying and then use the following 4 cords to tie the first row of Square Knots.

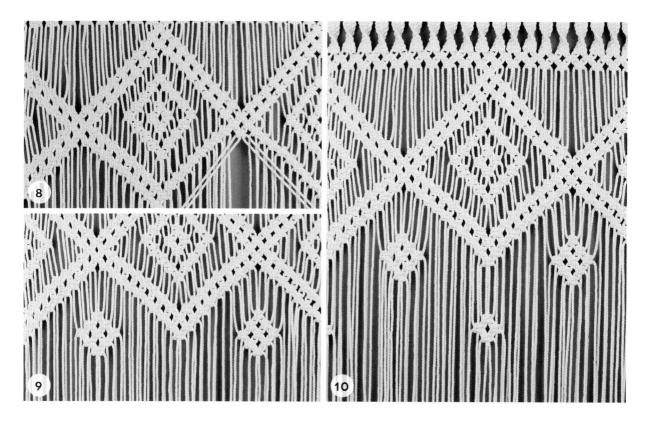

8. Once you have completed the 1st rows of Square Knots to close the diamonds, complete the 2nd rows. For each diamond, start the 2nd row of Square Knots using 2 of the cords in the middle where the diamonds join.

9. Make 4 Square Knot Big Clusters between the 4 diamonds in the center of the design. Leave a space of 3.2 inches (8 cm) from the pattern above and take the 4 cords in the middle to start the clusters.

10. Next, make 5 Square Knot Small Clusters at the bottom of the diamonds, leaving 3.2 inches (8 cm) from them. In order to begin the clusters, use the last 4 cords you used to make the last Square Knot of the diamonds. Finally, trim the ends at 31.5 inches (80 cm) from the dowel and unravel them a little bit.

SUMMER BREEZE CURTAIN

FINISHED SIZE
30 inches wide x 7.5 feet long (76 cm wide x 2.3 m long)

MATERIALS
Wooden dowel, 3.3 feet (1 m) long

3mm 3-strand twisted cotton cord, about 1,102 feet (336 m) total

CUTS
56 pieces, 20 feet (6 m) long

KNOTS & PATTERNS
Lark's Head Knot (page 16)

Square Knot (page 18)

Square Knot Diamond (page 34)

Square Knot with Multiple Filler Cords (page 20)

Square Knot Small Cluster (page 33)

You can't touch the air, but you can see how things move with it, and that is what we love about macramé curtains! The gentle movement of the cords and the sun rays that drift through them will take you back to a memorable summer afternoon.

This curtain is an excellent project for beginners who want to take risks and make big pieces to serve as decorative and practical items. You'll have lots of fun creating this lovely piece of art for your home!

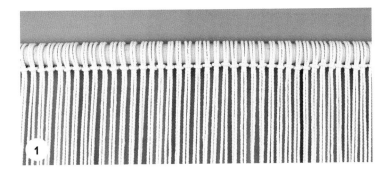

1. As you'll be working with very long cords, we suggest that you tape the ends so that they don't unravel as you go. Attach all 56 pieces of the 20-feet (6-m)-long cord onto the dowel with the Lark's Head Knot.

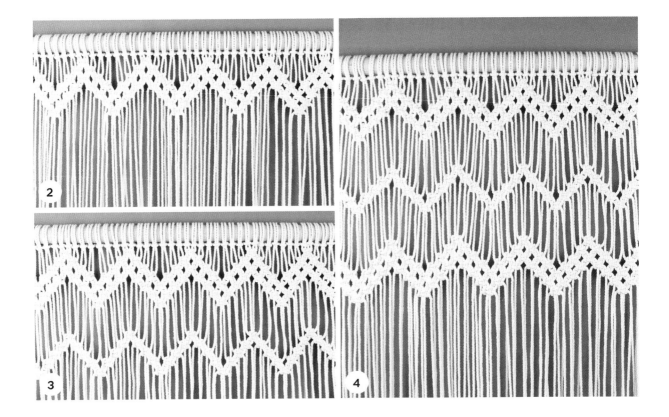

2. Begin the design from the left. Take cords 7, 8, 9 and 10 to start a Square Knot zig-zag pattern. Tie 3 Square Knots diagonally to both sides. Then, leave 12 cords counting from the 1st Square Knot you've done (that would be cords 13, 14, 15 and 16) and tie another Square Knot to continue with the zig-zag pattern, always leaving 12 cords in between. Repeat the same with the following cords. In order to make a double zig zag, tie another row of Square Knots.

3. Leave a space of 4 inches (10 cm) from the top part of the zig zag and tie a row of Square Knot zig zags as explained in step 2.

4. Repeat step 2, leaving a space of 4 inches (10 cm) again to make another zig zag of 2 rows.

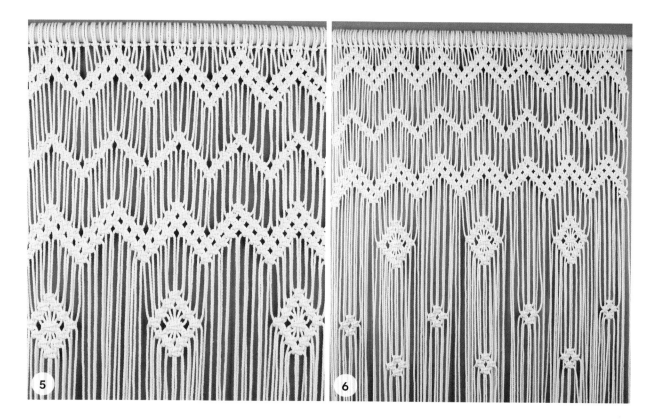

5. Starting from the left side of the design, leave a space of 4 inches (10 cm) from the top part of the last zig zag and take the cords 23, 24, 25 and 26 to tie a Square Knot Diamond of 4 knots with a Square Knot with Multiple Filler Cords inside it. Repeat the same procedure but this time with cords 55, 56, 57 and 58. Do the same with cords 87, 88, 89 and 90. You will get 3 Square Knot Diamonds.

6. Make 4 Square Knot Small Clusters. Start each of them using the 4 cords in the middle of the last zig-zag pattern, leaving 12 inches (30 cm) from the top part of the 1st, 3rd, 5th and 7th zig zags. Make 3 more Square Knot Small Clusters at 8 inches (20 cm) from the bottom part of the 3 diamonds. Start them using the 4 cords from the last Square Knot of the diamond.

Hang the curtain where you want to display it, and then trim the cords. This way you can cut the ends at the appropriate length to suit the space.

COZY RUG

If you are like us, you LOVE the coziness of rugs! They complete spaces and make them look elegant. The versatility of this rug makes it perfect for any room, but we placed it in the bedroom because the play between texture and simple design will feel like a massage for your feet when you get up!

You will enjoy the challenge of working with long cords and making a simple, attractive, decorative and useful piece for your home!

FINISHED SIZE
20 inches wide x 35.5 inches long (50 cm wide x 90 cm) long

MATERIALS
Wooden dowel, at least 27.5 inches (70 cm) long (only needed to knot the design, then taken off)

3mm 3-strand twisted cotton cord, about 558 feet (170 m) total

High-quality Scotch or masking tape

CUTS
36 pieces, 185 inches (470 cm) long

KNOTS & PATTERNS
Lark's Head Knot (page 16)

Alternating Square Knot (page 28)

Double Half Hitch Diamond Knot (page 35)

Square Knots Alternating Inner and Outer Cords (page 31)

1. As you'll be working with very long cords, we suggest that you tape the ends so that they don't unravel as you go. Attach all 36 pieces of the 185-inch (470-cm)-long cords onto the dowel with the Lark's Head Knot. You will only need to use the dowel to hang the design while knotting; once it is finished, you'll take the macramé off of the dowel.

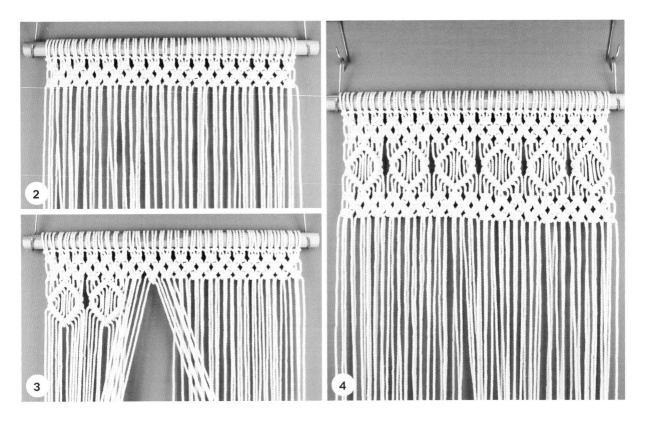

2. Start the design from the left and tie 3 rows of Alternating Square Knots.

4. Make 3 rows of Alternating Square Knots.

3. Now, you are going to make 6 Double Half Hitch Diamonds every 3 Square Knots. Take the first 3 Square Knots and use the 2 cords in the middle to start a Double Half Hitch Diamond. Repeat the same procedure with the remaining cords.

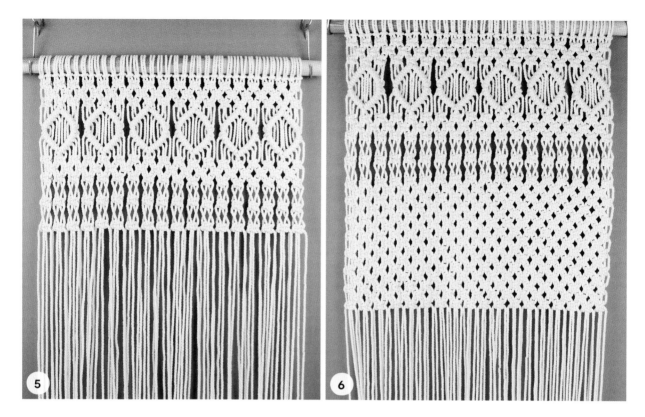

5. Then, leave a space of 1.2 inches (3 cm) and make a row of Square Knots, alternating the inner and outer cords. Repeat it once more.

6. Tie 14 rows of Alternating Square Knots. Try to tie them tight rather than loose so that it gives more structure to the rug.

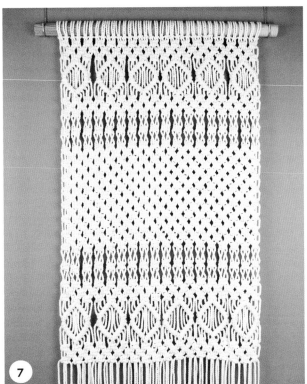

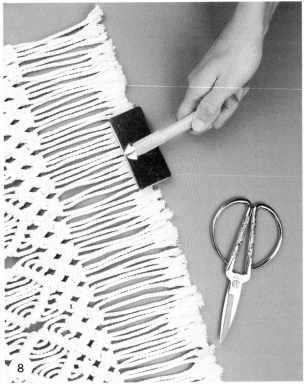

7. Now, you are in the middle of the rug. As it is a symmetric design, you will repeat what you have done at the beginning. Repeat step 5. Repeat step 2 to make 3 rows of Square Knots. Then, repeat step 3 to make a row of Double Half Hitch Diamonds. Finally, as in step 4, make 3 more rows of Square Knots.

8. The rug is ready! Take it off the dowel, trim both ends to be the same length and unravel them a little bit. See page 13 for tips about cleaning the rug if it becomes dirty from use.

On the Table

Setting the table is a ceremony that many people enjoy doing daily or for special occasions. If you are one of those people who are constantly looking for decorative details to amuse your loved ones and bring beauty to everyday moments, you are in the right place! There are an endless number of macramé accents you can make to decorate or to simply give a graceful touch to the table.

Here, we share with you some of our favorite projects: a lovely table mat (page 151), two breathtaking table runners (page 147 and 143) and an exquisite and warm jar lantern (page 157). All of these beautiful projects are so flexible that they are perfectly suitable for homes or for special events like weddings and birthdays.

So, come on! Give your table love with one, if not all, of these projects!

HARMONY TABLE RUNNER

Macramé and home décor are closely connected, so it is not a coincidence that we love them both! We really appreciate the harmony of those places where everything is taken into account to highlight the simplicity of things.

We designed a geometric pattern for this piece that helped us to create a symmetrical and awe-inspiring decorative accent for any table of the house. It's simple, delicate and stunning all at the same time!

FINISHED SIZE

6.25 feet long x 16 inches wide (1.9 m long x 40 cm) wide

MATERIALS

Wooden dowel, at least 24 inches (60 cm) long (only needed to knot the design, then taken off)

3mm 3-strand twisted cotton cord, about 590 feet (180 m)

CUTS

30 pieces, 236 inches (600 cm) long

KNOTS & PATTERNS

Lark's Head Knot (page 16)

Square Knot (page 18)

Increasing Alternating Square Knot (page 29)

Square Knot V-Shape (page 30)

Square Knot Diamond (page 34)

Decreasing Alternating Square Knot (page 29)

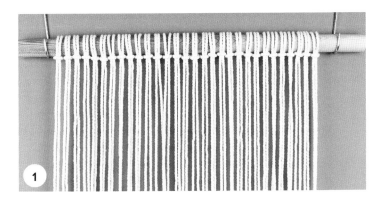

1. As you'll be working with very long cords, we suggest that you tape the ends so that they don't unravel as you go. Attach the 30 pieces of 236-inch (600-cm)-long cord onto a dowel with the Lark's Head Knot. You will only need to use the dowel to hang the design while knotting; once it is finished, you'll take the macramé off of the dowel.

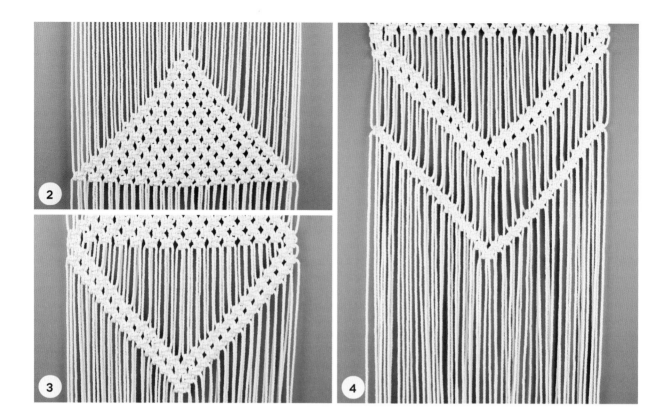

2. Leave a space of 12 inches (30 cm) and use cords 15, 16, 17 and 18 to tie a Square Knot. Use this 1st knot as the starting point and tie all the remaining cords with the Increasing Alternating Square Knot pattern until you reach the outer cords.

4. Take the outer cords, leave a space of 5 inches (12 cm) from the last pattern and tie another Square Knot V-shape row.

3. Take the outer cords to start tying a Square Knot V-shape. Tie Square Knots until you reach the middle of the design; those are cords 15, 16, 17 and 18. Repeat this procedure in order to get 2 rows.

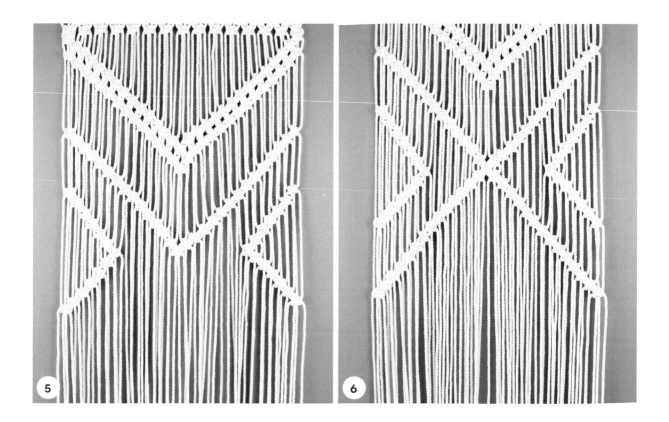

5. Staring from the outer part of the design, leave a space of 3.2 inches (8 cm) and tie a Half Square Knot Diamond of 7 knots. Repeat the same on the right side of the design.

6. Starting from the bottom of the V-shape you did in step 4, keep on knotting Square Knots diagonally in order to get an X design.

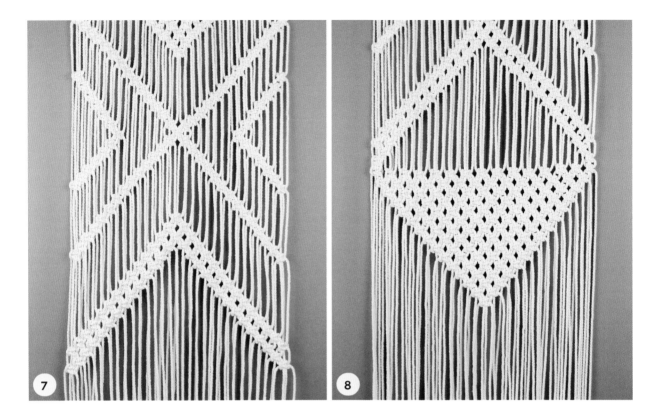

7. Take the 4 cords in the middle of the piece, leave a space of 5 inches (12 cm) from the previous design, and tie a Square Knot. Keep on tying Square Knots diagonally to both sides to create an inverted V-shape. Repeat this procedure in order to get 2 rows.

8. Now, in order to finish the design, you have to tie 1 complete row of Square Knots using all the cords. Then, start a decreasing pattern with Decreasing Alternating Square Knots until you only have 4 cords to make the last Square Knot.

Take the piece off the dowel and trim the ends at the same length, approximately 16 inches (40 cm) from the last design. Unravel the ends a little bit.

JOY TABLE RUNNER

Dressing the table is something that we love doing; it connects us with joy, love and sharing with family and friends. It's something that we intrinsically link to moments of celebration. So, we care about every detail to make it look appealing and to make our loved ones feel at home.

This table runner is ideal to give a distinctive style to your table. The natural beauty of a soft fabric combined with macramé gives you the opportunity to have fun working with different materials and, at the same time, create a piece for your home that you will definitely enjoy!

FINISHED SIZE
10 feet long x 16 inches wide (3 m long x 40 cm) wide

MATERIALS
Wooden dowel, at least 24 inches (60 cm) long (only needed to knot the design, then taken off)

5mm single-twist cotton string, about 394 feet (120 m) total

Linen fabric, 6 feet long x 16 inches wide (1.80 m long x 40 cm wide)

Nails

Sewing needle and thread

CUTS
60 pieces, 79 inches (200 cm) long

KNOTS & PATTERNS
Lark's Head Knot (page 16)

Square Knot (page 18)

Square Knot V-shape (page 30)

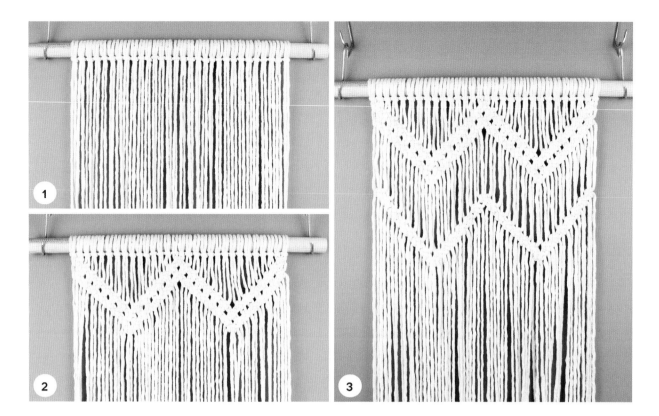

For this project you need to make 2 identical pieces.

1. Attach 30 pieces of the 79-inch (200-cm)-long cords onto the wooden dowel with the Lark's Head Knot. You will only need to use the dowel to hang the design while knotting; once it is finished, you'll take the macramé off of the dowel.

2. Begin the design by tying a Square Knot at the beginning, in the middle and at the end of the design. Take those Square Knots as the starting point for 2 V-shapes. Tie 6 Square Knots diagonally on each side and then 1 in the middle to finish it. Make 2 rows of Square Knots for each V-shape.

3. Leave a space of 4 inches (10 cm) and tie another row of Square Knots V-shape.

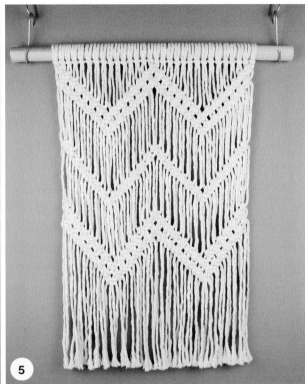

4. Leave a space of 4 inches (10 cm) and repeat step 2.

5. Trim the ends and slightly brush them. Then, take the piece off the dowel by holding the dowel on one of its ends and using the other hand to take cords off it one at a time. Use the same dowel to make the other piece.

Attach the macramé pieces on both ends of the fabric with nails. As these are bulky pieces, we suggest that you sew them by hand. Use the sewing needle and thread to carefully sew the cords to the fabric, one next to the other. After sewing, remove the nails.

NOTE: If you want to make it shorter, you can reduce the spaces in step 3 and use a shorter piece of fabric.

Namaste Table Mat

FINISHED SIZE

11 inches wide x 19 inches long
(27 cm wide x 48 cm long)

MATERIALS

Wooden dowel, at least
16 inches (40 cm) long (only
needed to knot the design,
then taken off)

5mm single-twist cotton
string, about 150 feet (45.8 m)
total

CUTS

18 pieces, 98.5 inches (250 cm)
long

2 pieces, 16 inches (40 cm) long

KNOTS & PATTERNS

Lark's Head Knot (page 16)

Double Half Hitch Knot
(page 21)

Diagonal Double Half Hitch
Knot (page 22)

Square Knot (page 18)

Square Knots Alternating
Inner and Outer Cords
(page 31)

This table mat is a delicate way of showing how much
we care about every single detail when it comes to
sharing special moments like teatime or a dinner with
loved ones.

It's elegant in its simplicity and a worthy project to
tackle if you would like a creative way to impress
guests at home. Don't hesitate in trying this fun-to-
make piece!

1. Attach the 18 pieces of 98.5-inch (250-cm)-long cords
onto the dowel with the Lark's Head Knot. You will only
need to use the dowel to hang the design while knotting;
once it is finished, you'll take the macramé off of the
dowel. Place 1 of the 16-inch (40-cm)-long cords over the
working cords and use it as a guide to tie a row of Double
Half Hitches. Remember to keep the guiding cord in
a horizontal position in order to make the pattern
look consistent.

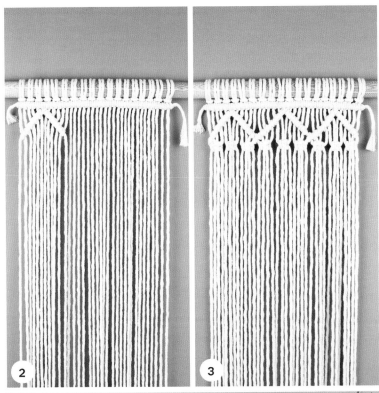

2. Start tying from the left. Take cords 5 and 6 and tie a Double Half Hitch Knot. Use both cords as guiding cords and tie 1 row of Diagonal Double Half Hitches to the left and 1 row to the right. Continue tying this zig-zag pattern by taking cords 18 and 19 and repeating the same procedure. Repeat the same, taking cords 30 and 31.

3. Tie 1 row of Square Knots.

4. Leave a space of 0.8 inch (2 cm) and tie a row of Square Knots, alternating the inner and outer cords. Tie 5 more rows in the same way, always leaving a space of 0.8 inch (2 cm) in between.

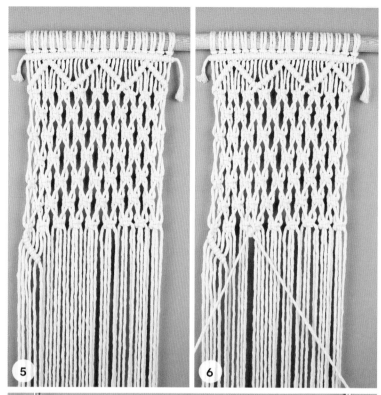

5. In order to tie a Double Half Hitch zig-zag pattern again, take the outer cord from the left and use it as a guide to tie a row of 5 Double Half Hitches.

6. Take cords 12 and 13 and tie a Double Half Hitch Knot. Use both cords as guiding cords and tie 1 row of Diagonal Double Half Hitches to the left and 1 row to the right.

7. Now, use cords 24 and 25 and repeat step 6. Take the outer cord from the right and use it as a guide to tie a row of 5 Double Half Hitches.

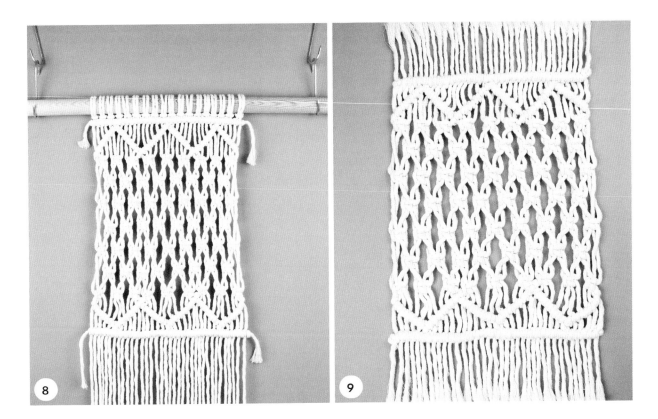

8. In order to finish the pattern, place the 2nd piece of 16-inch (40-cm)-long cord over the working cords and use it as a guide to tie a row of Double Half Hitches.

9. Take the mat off the dowel and trim the ends on both sides at the same length.

MOONLight JAR Lantern

10 inches (25.5 cm) high

This project is an absolutely delightful way to reuse extra glass jars you surely have at home. With this macramé design, you will transform a simple jar into a charming decorative object to light up your nights. The spaces between the cords allow light to gently pass through it, creating a pleasant and warm atmosphere.

You will also have the opportunity to experience working in a different way since the project is attached to the jar from the beginning. This is a lovely project to enjoy at home or give as a handmade present!

MATERIALS

5mm single-twist cotton string, about 170 feet (52 m) total

Glass jar, 10 inches (25.5 cm) high, 18 inches (45 cm) diameter

A nice candle

CUTS

1 piece, 85 inches (215 cm) long

29 pieces, 67 inches (170 cm) long

KNOTS & PATTERNS

Half Hitch Knot (page 17)

Lark's Head Knot (page 16)

Square Knot Sinnet (page 26)

Alternating Square Knot (page 28)

Square Knot (page 18)

Double Half Hitch Knot (page 21)

Diagonal Double Half Hitch Knot (page 22)

1. Attach the 1 piece of 85-inch (215-cm)-long cord around the jar and fix it with a Half Hitch Knot. The ends of the cords should be the same length since you will use them to tie the knots.

2. Use the Lark's Head Knot to attach the 29 pieces of 67-inch (170-cm)-long cord onto the cord you have just tied around the jar.

3. Start the design by taking every 4 cords and making 15 Square Knot Sinnets of 3 knots each.

4. In order to join the sinnets, make 2 rows of Alternating Square Knots.

5. Every 3 Square Knots, leave the first 2 and last 2 cords without tying and make a row of 2 Square Knots. Finally tie 1 Square Knot using the 4 cords in the middle in order to get a V-shape. Repeat this pattern all around the jar and you'll end up with 5 Square Knot V-shapes.

6. Take the 2 cords where the V-shapes join and tie a Double Half Hitch Knot.

7. Then, continue using those same cords as guiding cords and tie a row of Diagonal Double Half Hitches close to the Square Knots, until you reach the last Square Knot. Join the guiding cords from the Diagonal Double Half Hitches rows with a Double Half Hitch in the middle.

Up to this step, this design works well for shorter jars; simply trim and brush the cords to finish. For a tall jar, continue onto step 8.

8. Repeat steps 6 and 7 to tie another row of Diagonal Double Half Hitches.

9. Continue using the same guiding cords from step 8 and tying Double Half Hitches diagonally; join them in the middle with a Double Half Hitch Knot. Trim the ends at the jar's length and brush them.

ACKNOWLEDGMENTS

Writing this book has been an amazing and unforgettable experience that was possible thanks to our families' support, love and care. Our kids, who live among cords and entrepreneur moms—our biggest thanks goes to them, our most important creations. And of course, thank you to our life partners, who always believe in us and constantly encourage us to go for more.

When making such a big work, we felt the support of all those who are proud of us, sincerely wishing us the best and following our journey. For those, a big thanks!

Thanks to Page Street Publishing and the lovely team for choosing our work to show to the world and for giving value to handmade work and entrepreneurs from different cultures. Thanks for this unbelievable opportunity.

Last but not least, we also want to thank all those who believe in Port Macramé Studio and always reach out to us with grateful and kind words. And thank YOU for being here, reading our book and supporting our work!

About the Authors

Carolina and Mariela are Argentinean sisters and the co-creators of Port Macramé Studio. They have lived in Mallorca, Spain, since 2020 when they moved there searching for a radical change in their lives. They were both closely connected to crafts since they were little girls but they finally found in macramé the opportunity to show and spread their passion and love for handmade work. They feel it was a blessing to come across this beautiful art and they soon started sharing it with other people through in-person workshops and tutorial videos on social media. They have been teaching macramé and selling small, medium and large macramé pieces all around the world ever since. Their fine and simple style and their love for decoration is the perfect combination for their modern and delicate pieces.

Every day they try to enjoy and find a balance between the challenging tasks of being full-time moms and entrepreneurs. Their Instagram account is full of macramé pieces, ideas and tips, where anyone can get started in the world of macramé and meet an amazing community of makers.

BECOME PART OF OUR COMMUNITY ON INSTAGRAM: @PORTMACRAMESTUDIO

Index